Global Call
Centers

Global Call Centers

Achieving Outstanding Customer Service Across Cultures & Time Zones

Erik Granered

NICHOLAS BREALEY
INTERNATIONAL

BOSTON · LONDON

First published by Nicholas Brealey International in 2005

100 City Hall Plaza, Suite 501
Boston, MA 02108, USA
Tel: 888 BREALEY
Fax: (1) 617-523-3708

3–5 Spafield Street, Clerkenwell
London, EC1R 4QB, UK
Tel: +44-(0)-207-239-0360
Fax: +44-(0)-207-239-0370

www.nicholasbrealey.com

© 2005 by Erik Granered

Printed in the United States of America

08   07   06   05   04   1   2   3   4   5

ISBN: 1-904838-03-0

Library of Congress Cataloging-in-Publication Data

Granered, Erik, 1967-
Global call centers : achieving outstanding customer service across
cultures and time zones / Erik Granered.
    p.   cm.
Includes bibliographical references and index.
ISBN 1-904838-03-0
1. Call centers.   2. Call centers–Management.   3. Customer services.   I. Title.
HE8788.G73 2005
658.8'12–dc22   2004024909

Contents

Acknowledgments

This project started because I had the opportunity to develop classes in cross-cultural communication and call-center management while at WorldCom in 2001 and 2002. For that opportunity I am thankful to Shiloh Burnam, the manager who assigned me those tasks. Also, Tracy Baldwin's experience and enthusiasm were essential. Beyond Shiloh and Tracy, I had the opportunity to observe and work with some of the most dedicated and talented people I have ever met. I want to thank all the WorldCom people in Cary, North Carolina, Amsterdam, and elsewhere for everything you taught me.

I also wish to thank Dr. Gary Weaver at The American University in Washington, DC. Most of what I know about cross-cultural communication, I learned from him. I have tried to source things as accurately as possible throughout the book, but there is no citation system in the world that can give sufficient credit to a teacher who opens windows into yourself and gives you a passion for life-long learning in a subject.

I also owe gratitude to the Incoming Calls Management Institute for originally recognizing that I was on to something that was worth sharing with a larger audience.

Lastly, I want to thank Nicholas Brealey Publishing. In particular, Erika Heilman's continuous feedback, praise and censure was invaluable. At some point during this project, I heard on a radio show that if you ever want to write a book, you had better get yourself a good editor. I am pretty sure I had the best.

Foreword

I begin by making a comparison between foreign aid and the setting up of global call centers. Sometimes, the giving of foreign aid is so resented by many in the donor country that an unkind word or the failure to be suitably subservient from the recipient can result in a hostile reaction on the part of the donor. These ungrateful poor people, we seem to be saying, better keep quiet and take it if they want to receive foreign aid. Adding to the difficulty is that communication in foreign aid models is a one-way flow: when the West speaks, the rest of the world must listen. The only cultural voice of any relevance here is that of the foreign aid donor. What gets forgotten is the self-interest of the donor in giving aid, which is usually for strategic reasons, and the benefits of interactive communications that might make the foreign aid model effective.

The West is speaking again and this time the subject is offshoring and outsourcing, especially on the setting up of call centers in the developing world. The messages are loud and clear: "They are taking our jobs"; "They can't understand us when we call"; "We don't understand them when they speak"; "They are rude"; "They are thankless"; "They will reveal our financial and health secrets to the world"; "Why should we pay them when we have people looking for jobs here?" These sentiments are being voiced far and wide. In fact, both of the 2004 U.S. presidential candidates have distorted this particular issue. During the campaign, Senator John Kerry outright condemned outsourcing and often speaks of "outsourcing terrorism." The linking of a security threat with a highly charged term from international trade policy is dangerous demagoguery at best. As for President George W. Bush, in spite of empirical surveys showing that offshoring and outsourcing can save hundreds of million of dollars for firms or result in other positive externalities, when his Chairman of the Council of Economic Advisors made reference to such research, he was quickly made to retract his statements. Many shrill voices in our media and politics talk about the practice of outsourcing being a net drain from developed economies. Just like foreign aid!

Both scenarios above showcase a zero-sum world, with one-way communication, and a singular story to tell about itself. They specify clear-cut alternatives or binaries: one gives, the other receives; one's loss is the other one's gain; one side has wealth and professionalism, the other none. Contrast this now with the following two disparate examples from the everyday lives of people in different parts of the world:

- My nephew Ankit Maharaj Singh works for a major credit card firm's call center in Gurgao, India. He is one of the 300,000 call center workers in India. He loves his job. Where else in India, he asks, can a newly minted college graduate earn fourteen thousand rupees a few months after graduation? What is your job all about? "Customer service," he says. What type of cultural sensitivity training did you receive? He rattles off the usual list that includes quality of service, recognizing various types of accents in the United States and Europe, and learning to speak in a "neutral" Indian accent. "We don't have to practice American accents," he emphasizes to me. He says that only about 5 percent of their complaints are from people getting upset that they are speaking to someone in India. He speaks of e-learning software programs that help them locate cultural contexts of customers in the United States as they speak to them. Who are your toughest customers, I ask? "Indians in America," he fires back, before I have finished the question. "They cop such an attitude when they talk to us," he says.

- Johnny Rivera is the Telecommunications Manager for Western Union's Latin America Regional Operations Center on the outskirts of San José, Costa Rica. On a recent visit, he proudly showed me the high-tech, spacious, and neatly laid out space for the call center. When speaking to the advantages of Costa Rica, he notes that Costa Ricans are bilingual and can mediate between Spanish and English language cultures, apart from providing services within each language's cultures. He notes that Western Union closed down its call center in Belgium but the one in Costa Rica was seen as indispensable for the firm's hemispheric operations. Officials at CINDE, Costa

Rica's foreign investment promotion agency, and COMEX, the ministry of foreign trade, also speak to me enthusiastically of their hubs and spokes model, in which the U.S. economy is the hub and countries like Costa Rica are the spokes. However, speaking of the far-away future, Johnny Rivera conjectures that the time may come when Americans have to move for their jobs abroad rather than the other way round. I tell him that more than three million of them already do so.

The two "grassroots" stories above also have common features: they showcase people eager to fit into the global service economy, a world in which the "us" and the "them" are not so clearly defined and there are all kinds of communications—top-down, bottom-up, hierarchical, and networked. Compared to the view "from above," us and them seems to be a culture clash indeed!

It is in this culture clash of micro proportions that Erik Granered's *Global Call Centers* must be placed. He acknowledges that the need to communicate is universal but so is our fear of difference. When applying this to global call centers, he notes that there are no quick fixes. Call centers are intercultural interactions. This simple lesson is the book's strength and its starting point. In showing the dynamism of cultures, in taking a systems approach, and in underscoring the value of self-awareness, the book underscores crucial, often underemphasized, dimensions of call center training programs. The neglect of these dimensions can result in huge losses to corporations. This makes the book a *must-read*, rather than a should-read, for executives and students of culture.

Seeing the world through cultural and systemic lenses might perhaps reveal dimensions to the evolution of globalization that we may otherwise miss. Political hue and cry aside, globalization continues to thicken and deepen, often in unexpected ways. If you are a business manager, be aware of your biases in thinking of globalization in particular ways: as a world of us versus them rather than a world of many dimensions.

Erik Granered writes of a world in which call centers are everywhere— often catering to multiple markets, domestic and international. Here there are American firms catering to Chinese customers, Belgian firms catering to Australian customers, and Caribbean firms catering to European customers. Binaries and stereotypes are not going to help firms provide customer service effectively. This book speaks to both the theory as well as the practice of seeing cultures in systemic ways. With observations taken from Leonard Bernstein to Buddhism, *Global Call Centers* also makes for engaging reading and is written in an accessible manner.

The eagerness to fit and work in an interconnected global economy may come as a surprise to those in the United States who view globalization unfavorably. But, it offers a respite from the violence that mars our world and extends the vision of statesmen like Woodrow Wilson and Cordell Hull who equated multilateralism and international trade with peace. A worker in Ohio who has just lost her job to a call center in San José may find little solace in such ideals. To argue against globalization, however, may be throwing out the baby with the bathwater. Nor is globalization about to stop. *Global Call Centers* offers ways in which we can make such intercultural interactions less emotionally painful and more materially rewarding. After all, isn't it time the West woke up to the multidimensional multicultural world?

—J. P. Singh, Ph.D.,
     Communication, Culture and Technology Program,
     Georgetown University and author of
     *Leapfrogging Development? The Political Economy
     of Telecommunications Restructuring*

Introduction

I magine a world with perfect interpersonal communication, where everyone speaks the same language and every word means the same thing to every individual. Each person in this imaginary world has the same skill level and education. Perhaps, in this world, people even communicate telepathically with each other, like aliens in a science fiction movie. Now, imagine what call center operations would look like in this kind of world. A company could set up one call center for all issues and route all the calls to it. Customer service agents and customers would politely solve all problems in a matter of minutes, each party departing happily with his or her desired solution.

The world we live in is far from the picture presented above. As it is, we live on six continents, oceans apart; we speak thousands of different languages; and our experiences and our values are diverse. We are far apart in the areas of education and skill level as well. Yet despite all these differences, one thing we share universally is the need to communicate. Could you imagine living your life in complete isolation? One additional thing that we share with each other is that we all need a little help sometimes, even for simple things such as finding a phone number or reserving an airline ticket. And, when we need help, we often use technology to contact someone who can solve the problem.

That technology is advancing at a dizzying pace. The world continues to shrink as advances in technology bring people from far corners of the planet ever closer to each other. Telecommunications carriers have laid miles of fiber across the oceans and into our cities than we know what to do with. Developing countries are leapfrogging telephone access by using wireless technologies. Companies and countries deploy more and more advanced satellites into the sky as old ones become obsolete. The Internet is growing so fast that most of us have stopped tracking just how fast it is grow-ing. "The Net" has become so pervasive that we just assume everyone has access to it, although of course this is not the case worldwide.

Current trends in the call center industry are right in step with these broader trends. Companies are now outsourcing not only customer service functions to less expensive locations but also advanced white-collar jobs, just as we were outsourcing manufacturing jobs twenty years ago. Perhaps we should not be surprised. Immigrants in every developed and developing country have performed labor, often well and at low cost, for hundreds of years. In North America, in particular, the history of this trend is particu-larly obvious as waves of immigrants moved here in search of opportunity. Often, these opportunities were farm, factory, and service functions that used to be performed by the incumbent population. Beyond North Amer-ica, many of my friends in my native Sweden were the children of recent immigrants from Finland who had moved to find opportunity at the local steel mill. But today, technology is often allowing companies to bring tal-ents for certain functions closer to home, without requiring people to actu-ally move across the world.

This long-distance telecommuting presents its own set of challenges. Consider the situation of a Mexican immigrant sweeping floors at a hotel in New York and a college graduate from India answering computer questions over the phone. The major difference in these two situations has nothing to do with the education level or language skills of those involved; rather it has to do with the requirement to communicate. Sweeping floors requires little communication with the hotel patrons, whereas in a call center setting, one of the core competencies is to have effective communication skills. Sure, you may say, "That rep in Bangalore speaks English better than I do." How-ever, command of the language is not enough; there are major cultural dif-ferences that can still make interaction problematic. The same sets of challenges would be true if you took that Mexican immigrant and put him at the hotel front desk. Communicating clearly and effectively in a cross-cultural customer service setting is, at times, difficult. The good news is that these difficulties can largely be overcome through training.

Unfortunately, we often look for quick fixes to the obvious problems around us without truly understanding one another's perspective. For example, a call center outsourcing company provides its agents with a few weeks of accent neutralization training. Done, problem solved, right? Or, as another example, the manager in a New York office teaches his staff one word of Spanish: *basura* (trash). Why? Because "there's a new guy in building services, and all trash must be clearly marked for removal. Just think what would happen if that box of freshly printed full-color brochures was thrown out in error."

What a sad commentary. Is that really all I need to know about this person, who may very well live down the street from me—that his word for trash is *basura*? And is it really enough to neutralize the accent of the Indian agent to make him more understandable to the customer in Indiana? Well, at least it is a start—as long as you are aware that everything is not fine with these simple fixes. A little knowledge can be a dangerous thing if you outsource all your customer service to India just because some fancy consultant tells you that it is possible to neutralize an Indian person's accent to some level that is acceptable. Before long, you may see your customers defecting due to other unforeseen agent-customer interaction issues. And, when that happens, both you and your customers will wonder what is going on. So too if you think that knowing the word *basura* will be sufficient when soon nearly half the population's primary language will be Spanish.

These examples are extreme, but if you are a customer service executive living in a shrinking world, you need to be sophisticated about the world around you. There is nothing wrong with accent neutralization, knowing the word *basura*, or any other words of convenience, for that matter. But in order to create a successful global call center infrastructure, you need a framework for understanding cultural differences. Why? Because if you do not have that knowledge, you will make bad decisions. You will open up a call center in the wrong place with untrained agents talking to your best customers. If you know what you are doing, you will open up a call center in the right place, strategically train your agents with measurable positive outcomes, and ensure that they are talking to the appropriate customer segment. In this scenario, you have lowered your costs, improved customer service, and earned praise as the customer service hero in your company.

✳   ✳   ✳

Global Call Centers is intended for thoughtful call center managers and executives who are genuinely interested in creating world-class customer service. On an intuitive level, it may appear obvious that world-class customer service is more important in some industries than in others. Let's say you are a businessperson who travels frequently. You probably get world-class customer service from your favorite airline once you identify yourself as a member of the "Frequent Flyer Business Class Club." But, when you have a billing question on your mobile phone, the response is not quite the same, is it? On a surface level, it may appear that culture as a strategic differentiator is more important to the former situation than the latter. It is, until we explore the concept of customer experience, add cost to the equation, and begin to look holistically at the myriad of options in creating your call center infrastructure. Then, we will discover that culture is a variable to be considered no matter what your industry or your desired service level.

Unfortunately, a sizeable portion of call centers are commonly known as "high-tech sweatshops." Such operations hire "junk-yard dogs" for managers, gladly tolerate employee turnover rates of 40 percent or more, and view training as an unfortunate means to an end. If you are in this category, you stand the most to gain from reading this book. Well-managed operations in the right location will beat miserable operations every time from every perspective. So, even if this cross-cultural stuff is of little interest to you, please read on for a purely business perspective.

On the other hand, if the concepts of cultural awareness and, even better, cultural fluency spark your interest, you will learn how cultural knowledge and awareness must trickle down from executive and management levels. Mechanisms must be created for this awareness to be spread to every employee. With this in mind, *Global Call Centers* is designed to serve as a training manual, filled with practical training tips to help you spread the awareness across your organization. It is my firm belief that this book can help you lower your costs and improve customer service simultaneously. This will be done by

- helping you make better decisions about where to locate your call centers;

- providing a deeper understanding of the dynamics of cross-cultural interaction;
- giving agents techniques for dealing with frustration, to reduce the burnout rate;
- providing tools for creating a positive customer-service culture in your center that is appropriate for the audience you are servicing;
- selecting agent incentives that are culture-appropriate; and
- revealing the ultimate role of the call center manager.

Part I of the book aims to create a knowledge base of how culture, the context in which we live and work, impacts human interaction. The central theme is that communication style is culturally determined. Our cultural differences create many opportunities for misunderstanding. Very simply put, when you talk to someone who is from the same cultural background as you are, you are both playing by the same rulebook. You have similar expectations regarding how the conversation is supposed to progress. When people from different cultural backgrounds interact, the potential for friction exists when a person expects one response and instead receives another.

This friction can lead to further miscommunication, and the consequence comes in the form of various kinds of emotional pain. Emotional pain is a theme that at first glance may appear too dramatic for the call center setting. It is my assertion, however, that emotional pain is at the crux of most, if not all, customer service problems.

Certainly there are degrees of emotional pain. If your agent has to withstand severe verbal abuse, this will clearly cause emotional pain. Anecdotally, call center managers know that the pain threshold for agents varies greatly. Some balk at any kind of frustration and march home in tears after only a few days of dealing with angry customers who either scream at them or hang up. Others take the interpersonal challenges in stride. The best customer service agents even feed on the ability to handle difficult situations well. Of course, the customer has a pain threshold as well. If a customer is just slightly irritated because your product does not perform as expected, the irritation is still a form of emotional pain, though on a smaller scale. But then again, did you ever yell at a customer service agent or just hang up in disgust? This response is so basic—a fight-or-flight response to perceived pain.

Part I also addresses the different modes of customer interaction, from written communication in the form of your documentation, to Web sites and chat rooms, to telephone conversations, and, last, to face-to-face meetings with your customers. All interactions are fraught with their own opportunities for creating misunderstanding and conflict. Knowledge and awareness are the keys to diffusing these moments of conflict. There is a method to the human madness of action and reaction; we push one another's buttons instinctively. Once we are aware of that cycle of behavior and understand what motivates the person on the other end, tremendous healing and coping powers are created inside the individual.

Once we shine the light on culture as a very real issue in call center interaction, we are ready to move on to Part II. Here you will find practical management strategies to create an atmosphere in your call center that resonates with the customer. You will discover how to use your training department as a strategic tool for creating a customer service culture in your center—no matter where it is located—that matches your customers' expectations, no matter where *they* are located.

Part III is designed as a reference tool and is a series of country studies. For ease of use, it is divided primarily along language lines, as language is often the main consideration in deciding where to locate a call center. These studies provide a deeper understanding of motivational and behavioral variables country by country. Some of these cultural traits are useful in deciding where to locate your call center and also in coaching agents on what to expect when dealing with specific cultural groups. From experience, I know that reading about your own cultural traits can cause quite a stir, both inside yourself and in spirited discussions that take place in group settings. Still, I encourage you to study your own cultural traits first. Honest self-awareness is the first step in creating effective cross-cultural communication. It follows that cultural self-awareness is important for effective management and decision making as well.

There are no quick and easy answers in this regard, and Part III cannot propose to be an exhaustive reference of cultural traits and their impact on call center communication. Please use Part II as a guide for how to leverage the country-specific information in Part III. By the time you reach Part III, you will have read many times that cultural awareness must cascade across your operations on a continuous basis through learning. Please study the training tips carefully so that your outcomes can be productive and positive.

Author's Note

Over my career, I have worked in organizational communication, marketing communication, and various kinds of communication training for customer service, leadership, and cross-cultural skills development. For me, communication is more than a major theme in this book or something that I do for a living. I view everything—from management, leadership, and learning, to raising children and community relations—as a communication process. In this book, I draw on fundamentals in the nature of human interaction to improve the opportunity to create a great customer service experience in the call center setting.

We are all human and we are all different. And we humans have gotten really good at figuring out how we are different from one another. We classify one another using genealogy, psychology, astrology, and anthropology. We use various tests and inventories to expose how different we are. There is nothing inherently wrong with any of those approaches. However, there is a fundamental problem that underlies all this abstracting, defining, and classifying. They often cause us to fail to see the true beauty and joy in difference, variety, and diversity itself.

Whether we like to admit it, we humans have a tendency to see *different* as *dangerous*. There are all kinds of negative implications that happen as a result of that reaction, mostly related to various flavors of fear. It is not my intent to leave you hanging here, because everything you read from here on is an attempt to resolve that dilemma.

Learning to engage constructively in the call center setting is not two-dimensional business challenge. Customer Relationship Management (CRM) tries to abstract the process into a science in which every step is controlled. This process can be very helpful in ensuring that the right information gets to the right customer and that issues are resolved. However, intended or not, the impact of that process is abstract and dehumanizing. To me, the ultimate CRM system is the small-town general store where the owner knows everyone in the town by name and understands all of their purchasing patterns. A romantic notion, perhaps, but you must agree that racks of computers and fancy software logic are just no substitute for that intimate experience.

I admit that I was once fascinated by The Peppers and Rogers Group's one-to-one customer service theories, which essentially see technology as a way to make interaction more intimate and efficient by using data-mining to learn more about the individual customer: technology as a means to an end. To the extent that this can be done, I support it completely, and later in the book I will speculate on how technology might some day bring us closer to the small-town general store experience.

Let me emphasize that many of the points made in this book are useful whether you are running international call center operations or something on a smaller scale. Cultural variations exist between domestic groups and between individuals within every group, and, therefore, what you will learn is relevant for all those seeking to create a satisfying customer experience. Learning about and appreciating our differences is valuable in any organizational setting. I hope you will find, as I have found, that nowhere do we have a greater opportunity for having a positive impact than in the call center, where technology is enabling human interaction on a massive scale—across the globe, every minute of every hour.

Share Your Experience

Some of the observations I have made in the book may seem more obvious than others. In fact, I expect that some of my assertions and recommendations might strike some readers as controversial. I trust that, as every organization is unique, there are approaches being applied that I have never heard of. In any case, I have set up an online bulletin board where you can post your reactions. I encourage you to share your experiences and your thoughts with me—and the call center community at large—at http:www.granered.net/bookblog. I can also be reached at http://gcc.granered.net

Part I

Global Call Centers:
The Customer Experience

It looks as though it's phoned in from God! Every note is perfect.

Leonard Bernstein describing Beethoven's compositions

1

Offshoring and Outsourcing

You've no doubt heard the terms *outsourcing* and *offshoring* bandied about in the headlines. Hardly a day goes by when the practice of outsourcing doesn't get picked up by the international media, even if only for its political currency. Indeed your company may already be actively employing some outsourcing options, perhaps even offshore. You may be on the cutting edge of this trend, or you may be just now contemplating these business models as a means of staying competitive. But what does it all mean—this business of business process outsourcing?

Efficiency at the Core

At the very core of business process outsourcing is the concept of efficiency. In this lightning-speed world, we are obsessed with doing things better, faster, and simpler. Efficiencies reduce cost, and in the final analysis we define efficiency in monetary terms. We also define efficiency in terms of time, but time and money are so closely linked that there can be little distinction between the two in the context of efficiency. If you can make something quicker, it reduces cost, and you make more money. But we must remember that efficiency cannot come at the expense of quality, since poor quality usually has a very negative financial impact in the long run.

Though it may not mark the beginning of mankind's obsession with efficiency, the modern concept of efficiency was formulated in the early 1800s by a British philosopher of utilitarianism, Jeremy Bentham. However, Nicols Fox, author of *The Hidden Luddite Tradition in Literature, Art and Individual Lives* and a forthcoming book on efficiency, finds that the real culprit is Frederick W. Taylor, who is commonly known as the father of scientific management, efficiency, and systems engineering. Working in the late nineteenth and early twentieth centuries, he divided tasks into specific actions and applied his stopwatch, attempting to demonstrate that the lazy rhythms of workers, left over from artisan days, could be efficiently reformed by the application of fractionated time analysis. "In the past," said Taylor, ominously, "the man has been first; in the future the system must be first" (Fox 2004).

It is not enough to be efficient in the here and now. You must continuously become more so, or others who are becoming so will soon put you out of business. In the midst of this never-ending quest for efficiency, business managers break everything down into components to ensure that each one is done right with minimum effort or resources applied. If something can be done with similar quality for less money (or more quickly), then you outsource that work and pocket the difference. However, savvy business managers do not perform this operational analysis in a vacuum. They remember to consider the sometimes hidden relationships between the individual components and consider the potential pitfalls as well as the benefits of physically fractionating their operation.

Outsourcing versus Offshoring

The term *outsourcing* is an umbrella term that refers to contracting out a set function to another company that specializes in that work: in our case, call center operations. The terms *nearshoring* and *offshoring* refer to locating these functions abroad, whether near or far. Nearshoring and offshoring can also involve outsourcing, or they can be done through wholly owned operations or a hybrid model. Complicated? No, not really, and we don't have to get too hung up the terminology or its meaning. The key point here is that regardless of whether you operate a call center in India or Israel,

no wonder, as it's changing rapidly each day. Its birth and growth is closely linked with the growth of consumerism and economic growth in the industrialized world. That is not to say that there were no call centers in other parts of the world until recently. Of course there were, but the mass adoption of consumer goods such as the car, the radio, the television, and the computer, combined with an obsession with customer service, has been the driving force in creating call center innovation. One of the primary areas of innovation has been in the application of computer technology. Today, telephone and computer technologies are so deeply intertwined that is difficult to see where one ends and the other begins. Telephone routing is completely done by computers even for calls that travel over old copper wires and that are placed with traditional rotary phones.

One important piece of computer technology used to support call centers is the Automatic Call Distributor, or ACD. These machines have become central to call center operations and will be referred to frequently in the rest of this book. There are many vendors who make them, and they range from fairly basic to extremely fancy and often expensive pieces of equipment. At its core, an ACD is a computer that connects to the telephone lines (also referred to as the "trunk") at their point of entry into the business location. Using resident software, the computer applies preset rules as to how calls are routed. It is via the ACD that businesses can do such things as

- *call routing based on call origin.* The ACD can be configured to route calls from the United States to a call center in Bangalore, as the ACD can usually detect the place of origin of a call. Or the ACD might route those U.S. calls to Dallas until 8 P.M., at which time they are routed to Bangalore for 24/7 coverage.
- *call routing based on interactive voice response (IVR).* This is probably the most prevalent and obvious of the ACD functions. Here the ACD picks up the call and gives the caller a list of options, which may be responded to by pushing keys or by giving verbal responses to prompts.
- *call routing based on skill (Skill-Based Routing).* This type of routing relates closely to the Interactive Voice Response, but it can be much more complex than the obvious example of "press one to continue in English" or *"prensa dos para el español."* The IVR can be programmed

to determine how important the call is and to ensure the important calls get high-priority service in person. Low priorities may get computer-generated answers or be given the option to leave a message. There are virtually no limits as to how intricate and complex the scenarios can be. But to be sure, *complex* is not always the same as *superior* from the perspective of the customer.

- *call queuing*. It is the ACD that puts us on hold and plays lovely music until an agent becomes available. This lineup is called a queue. The reason you are put on hold will depend on many factors. It boils down to whether an agent who has the skills and resources to deal with your issue is available at this particular time. Remember that the ACD decides how to handle your call based call origin, IVR selections, time of day, and agent availability. The next time you get put on hold, don't get mad at the ACD, though. Somebody at the call center configured it, and somebody at the company you are calling decided how may agents it could afford to make available.

Virtually anything you can imagine the ACD can do, with the help of the ingenuity of the vendors who make them and the phone companies that provide the trunk. I offer this little technology briefing here because when you understand how calls can be handled, your imagination can truly begin to run free with creative schemes for who does what, where, and when for maximum efficiency. What experts discovered rather quickly in the evolution of call centers was that the theory of economies of scale applied to call center operations in a relevant way. In other words, large call centers handling significant call volume are much more efficient than small call centers handling a variety of issues—*efficient* meaning more calls can be handled with relatively fewer resources.

This is a universal truth that has resulted in what we might call the U.S. model of call center operations. Two events, one technological and one legislative, have significantly contributed to enabling large call center operations to proliferate across America. First, AT&T developed toll-free service, allowing charges to be reversed. Then a ruling by the United States Federal Communications Commission stated that equipment other than that made by Bell Systems would be allowed on the public networks. The innovation that resulted eventually led to the ACD as we know it today. This technological evolution, along with the use of vanity customer-support telephone numbers such as 1-800-FLOWERS, created growth. According to Datamonitor, there were about eighty thousand call centers in the United States by 1998 (*Call Center Magazine* 2000), many of which were located in places such as Omaha, Nebraska, or Saint Louis, Missouri, because they offered high-quality labor at a reasonable cost.

Countries that first began attracting call center operations to handle American customer inquiries included Ireland and Israel. When this offshoring started, these countries shared some important traits with today's booming call center host, India, in that they offered an abundance of highly skilled workers who spoke English and were willing to work for a comparatively low wage. Early movers to these offshore locations were American companies with global operations that demanded a high level of service availability, including such travel-related industries as hotel companies and airlines. High-tech companies soon followed as they saw the savings and the quality of service. The Irish and Israeli markets are now relatively saturated and labor rates in Ireland have increased to the point that it is not the glaring value proposition that it used to be.

The Current State of the Industry

Reports and articles abound that attempt to create a realistic picture of what is happening in the call center industry, some with more reliability than others. One of the best sources of data and analysis about the call center industry comes from the U.K.-based research company Datamonitor. They produce very detailed reports about the industry, usually by geographic region. The full reports are expensive; however; because good information is so critical in making key decisions, such as where to locate a call center, they can be well worth the price. Forrester Research, IDC, and Gartner Group are other firms that also provide industry research on the subject.

Consider the following facts:

- The number of people who work in call centers worldwide is estimated at 4.78 million, 2.82 million of whom are in the United States (Datamonitor 2004).

- The number of people working in call centers in all of Europe, the Middle East and Africa (EMEA) is forecasted to exceed 2 million employees by 2008 (Datamonitor 2004).
- Offshoring is predicted to grow at a rate of 30 to 40 percent a year for the next several years (McKinsey Global Institute 2003).
- By 2015 as many as 3.3 million U.S. jobs and $136 billion in wages could be moved to such countries as India, China, and Russia (McCarthy 2004).

These facts indicate that there has been a real trend toward offshoring, not just in the call center industry, but overall. Further, indications are that this phenomenon is not some temporary trend that will go away when everyone realizes that folks in India and other places are, and remain, culturally different than us. The need to reduce cost is the main driving force in the call center world. This was always the case, but it still is as true today. Outsourcing tends to reduce cost; that is why Datamonitor predicts that the market for outsourced voice services will reach 76.5 million by 2005 (Datamonitor 2004).

The offshore call center operation business has also benefited from "mistakes" in other industries. In the late 1900s there was an overbuilding of the capacity for telecommunications between the continents that has resulted in drastic reductions in the cost of international telephone links. This cost reduction in fiber optic links around the world is enabling the offshoring trend. Prices have fallen by 80 percent since 1998. It is a simple case of supply and demand. Excess supply reduces prices. Capacity to carry voice and data to India alone grew sevenfold between 2001 and 2002. It will double again between 2004 and 2005 (Drucker 2004).

As mentioned earlier in our discussion of ACD systems, companies continue to look to technology to create competitive advantage in the form of reduced cost and better service. According to a February 2004 report by Datamonitor, companies spent a staggering $695 million on "workforce optimization technologies" in 2003, and this trend continues to grow at a very healthy pace. Technologies that manage the customer-relations process include trouble ticketing systems, ACD systems, and agent monitoring systems. Other areas of innovation include voice over IP, speech recognition, and blended service approaches using voice, web, and chat.

All of this points to the fact that call centers are truly a global industry. You could put a call center nearly anywhere in the world, depending on your needs. This means that the decision regarding where to locate it is complex.

A recent write-up in the *Wall Street Journal* about Sykes Industries, a company that had become a success in the late 1990s by building up call centers in rural areas in places such as Kentucky and North Dakota, reveals some interesting clues about current trends in the industry (Morse 2004). American workers are as mobile as any worker anywhere. They are willing to relocate to where the jobs are. The beauty of building call centers in rural areas was that everyone was happy. Workers did not have to move, and call centers got skilled labor at reasonable prices. As it turns out, the business processes themselves are even more mobile than the employees.

In early 2000, Sykes issued a profit warning and the stock plummeted. Customers were demanding lower cost. Keep in mind, however, that Sykes was operating a rather lean business as it was. Facilities had been set up with generous local incentives. Sykes was benefiting from plummeting telecom costs as everyone else was, and workers in rural America were making about minimum wage fielding calls.

Sykes had started building up call centers around the world earlier, but by 2004, less than four years after the profit warning, more than half of the North American call centers had been closed or were due to close shortly, with the jobs set to be relocated to the Philippines, China, and Costa Rica (Morse 2004). This is just one example of the offshoring trend, but certainly there are many more like this one.

Economic and Political Impact of Offshoring

Outsourcing manufacturing jobs to low-cost countries has been an ongoing trend for decades and shows no signs of slowing down. The truth is that world leaders are scrambling every day to open up markets and reduce the barriers to outsourcing despite some public protests and despite the threat of international terrorism.

Does anyone remember rock star Bono of U2 fame and then–U.S. Treasury Secretary Paul O'Neal touting the wonderful work of an insurance company that had outsourced claims processing to Accra, Ghana? The year was 2002, and Bono was speaking on behalf of global openness. Certainly, Bono must have been aware of the enormous contribution call center outsourcing had made to the economic development in his native Ireland. Why could this not happen in Accra as well? Skilled workers, relatively stable politics, and incentives from a pro-investment government were all conditions similar to Ireland fifteen years ago. Why not? Indeed, why not.

A year later, Bono was in Seattle condemning globalization and its wide-ranging effects. The loss of higher-quality jobs to foreign countries is an explosive issue in the United States and elsewhere. From the perspective of developing countries it can be explosive as well. In Mexico, workers who have been doing entry-level manufacturing work are losing their jobs to workers in China. That, in turn, is forcing Mexican companies to transition their capabilities toward higher-end manufacturing, such as making routers and other advanced electronic gear that used to be made in the United States.

Economically, we have grown accustomed to paying ever-lower prices for things we need or think we want at super-sized stores out in the suburbs. Wal-Mart is conditioning us to "watch for ever-falling prices," as each commercial cheerily says. Companies operating in this environment have to take advantage of economic openness in order to stay competitive. That means they have to constantly seek new ways to become more efficient. These days, that means increasingly more advanced tasks are being done in places where labor costs are much lower than they are in the United States or in Europe. In fact, an ironic twist in the quest to outsource is that sometimes it is cheaper to allow inexpensive human labor to carry out tasks that used to be automated with conveyors. One white-goods company is making appliances in China without the aid of conveyors. It is less expensive to hire people to push the partially finished goods along the Chinese assembly line than to automate that process (*Washington Post* 2004).

Politically, the loss of high-quality jobs is controversial and generally disruptive to the perception of a healthy economy. The manufacturing sector, in particular, has suffered blow after blow with jobs going to lower-wage countries. It is ironic to watch the same politicians who have promoted and endorsed free trade for a lifetime now revolt and call for action to address the hemorrhaging of high-quality jobs. What did they think was going to happen? The historical perspective should be fairly clear here. We have already witnessed the emergence of Japan, Korea, Taiwan, and other countries as they made the transition from low-level manufacturing to more advanced functions. It is as if some kind of unspoken arrogance had lulled us into thinking that could never *really* happen in China or India. Well, it has. Two giants, each with about a billion people, are steadily and deliberately turning out highly skilled workers and putting them to work.

Solutions being presented to reverse the job loss range from reversing free trade agreements to taxing companies that decide to move overseas. One piece of proposed U.S. legislation, for example, would force customer service agents to reveal their location as an indirect disincentive to offshoring. This particular idea would do very little to slow the trend toward offshoring, in my opinion. As consumers, we already know when we are not speaking with a native speaker. There is no hiding the fact no matter how much accent neutralization training is provided. Knowing that there is a real likelihood that we will speak with somebody who has an accent, do we still call? Yes. Do we boycott companies that offshore customer service? Not to any tangible extent as far as I have seen. To the contrary, I contend that many consumers would be most interested to find out where the agent is located, sparking all kinds of interesting conversations to the call center manager's dismay, as talk-times—the amount of time an agent spends with an individual customer—would increase.

Can you picture it now?

Hello, thank you for calling ABC Phone Company, this is Raj. I am in Bangalore, how can I help you?

Hello Raj. Bangalore, huh? I hear it is beautiful there. Is it true the weather is much like it is in California?

Yes, very beautiful here. Can I answer any questions about your phone bill?

Yes, I have a cousin who is a computer programmer. He spent six months in Bangalore, and he loved it!

And so on . . . little chit-chat like that adds up. At an average of thirty seconds of added chit-chat per call, multiplied by one thousand calls per day, you have about eight hours of added talk-time per day. ABC Phone Company would have to add one additional full-time employee, probably more, to account for the additional time.

If any legislation is passed to slow down the outsourcing trend, who would pay for the additional cost? That is hard to say, but it could be you and me as the consumers. Remember, however, why the company wants to outsource and offshore in the first place — to reduce cost. Any disincentive to offshoring, then, does not add cost. It merely reduces the company's flexibility in the ongoing effort to reduce cost.

On the political front, it is unlikely that we will see legislation to slow offshoring that has real teeth. The companies that are benefiting from the low labor costs and that want to continue to ship jobs overseas are organizing to fight any legislative effort to slow the trend of offshoring.

Culture as a Success Factor

As we've seen, it is easy to make a case for outsourcing. Wages can be as low as one tenth of the equivalent wage in North America. The skill levels of the workers are often very high, since workers with university degrees are willing to take call center jobs in places such as India or the Philippines. In addition, you often have lower turnover because employees are actually happy to have a well-paying job, and the proposition becomes nearly irresistible.

For many companies, the decision to outsource customer service appears desirable at first glance. It did to Dell, which laid off thousands of support staff in Texas and routed the calls to India. Dell was a pioneer in offshoring customer service in 2000 and 2001, as it reacted to the economic downturn with cost-cutting measures. Beyond revolutionizing the manufacture of personal computers, Dell enjoyed a reputation as a company that provided excellent customer support. For whatever reason, many of Dell's customers were not happy to speak with their new customer service representatives in India. Stories of thick accents, long wait times, incompetence, rudeness, and more incompetence were rampant. It did not come as a surprise, then, that Dell started backtracking and routing calls back to Texas in November of 2003 for most of its business customers. Yet, the lure of the cost savings was still too strong to resist, as Dell decided to keep its Indian operations and work on improving operations there rather than completely reversing course. Calls from individual customers, which account for 15 percent of Dell's business, continue to be routed to India. The long-term success of this decision remains to be seen.

Dell is not the only company to backtrack on its customer service offshoring. Lehman Brothers, the financial brokerage house, outsourced internal help-desk functions to Wipro Spectramind, a very reputable vendor in India. Like Dell, Lehman had to reverse its move as U.S. employees were up in arms over the agents' lack of technical skill and their excessive tendency to stick rigidly to scripted responses. The size of Lehman's deal with Wipro was fairly small. There is speculation that it affected less than one hundred agents. The work was part of a larger contract in information technology services. Both Wipro and Lehman have been very tight-lipped about the motivation behind the decision to reverse offshoring, other than stating that the quality of service was low (*India Times*, December 13, 2003).

So it's reasonable to say that not every venture to lower cost through offshoring is a success. Another example of an experiment gone awry is the consumer goods company Shop Direct, which opened a call center in Bangalore employing 250 agents. Shop Direct is an online catalog and shopping hub that employs one thousand two hundred people in Leeds, United Kingdom. The decision to bring the work back home was based on the customer-perceived quality of service provided by Indian agents. A company spokesperson said, "They may be cheaper but I can certainly tell the difference when I am being served by someone overseas" (*India Times*, January 26, 2004).

Realistically, it often takes many rounds of trying before companies get it right. The stakes are high. Sure, you want to lower labor costs, but there are costs associated with reducing costs, that you may not even anticipate without expert help at your side. As a useful exercise, I encourage all customer service managers to go to their favorite Internet search engine and type in the name of your company and a phrase like "customer complaints." What you are likely to find, especially if your business deals with any kind of consumer product or business service, is a plethora of postings from livid customers.

To illustrate the point, here are some examples of quotations regarding one company that outsourced customer service (the specific product, company names, and locations have been omitted):

> *I then requested to speak a supervisor and ten minutes later I was talking to her. She was rude, spoke over me when I attempted to speak and told me that if I did not pay, she would issue a report that would damage my credit rating.*

> *Your company needs to rethink its policy of moving the highly important function of customer relations to disinterested people thousands of miles away.*

> *Their so-called customer service (no doubt) is the worst in this world. I have never had to deal with such awful service from a self centered, domineering, egotistical, feeble-minded, bull-headed, two faced, chronically maladaptive, unorganized piece of you-know-what in my life! So many times I would be on hold well over one hour before those dumb reps would finally decide to answer the call.*

And, unfortunately, there is plenty more where that came from.

To summarize, there are tangible consequences for not considering cultural variables at every stage of outsourcing and offshoring call center functions. Beyond wasting company resources on ventures that might fail, you could harm your company's reputation, which, in turn, could affect the bottom line. There are both strategic and tactical implications in deciding which customer segment is served by which call center and how agents are trained to handle customer issues. Your company earns its reputation not only on what its product quality and prices are, but on how it behaves as a corporate citizen, as a member of society at large.

Human Consequences and Public Relations

My purpose in writing this book is not to advocate for or against the relentless cost-cutting practice of outsourcing, though I clearly show a bias in how to properly handle the process. Let's be blunt. Offshoring causes a lot of stress and disruption for the individuals and families affected. There is probably nothing, barring health problems or death, that is as stressful and unsettling as having a family—and all the incumbent trappings—without having a job to sustain them. Still, with all the shifting business models around us, I offer up a solution: As a society and as individuals we can handle such changes with compassion. When people lose their jobs to foreign, lower-wage workers, we can offer some time for the transition to take hold. We must realize that the hardship of losing one's job is not an acceptable price of progress. Retraining affected workers to be successful in other jobs seems the right thing to do not only for the individual but for the economy and society in general. The political debate should start not with whether retraining and support are needed but rather with who pays for it and what new skills training should be offered.

In February of 2004, Hewlett-Packard announced that it had set up call center operations in Bangalore to handle calls related to its consumer products such as PCs, printers, and digital cameras. On almost exactly the same day the announcement came out, a letter from HP Chairwoman Carly Fiorina appeared on the op-ed page of the *Wall Street Journal* (Fiorina 2004). In the article, Fiorina makes an argument to the effect that the world so very competitive that "there is no job that is America's God-given right anymore." The press release stated that no American jobs were lost in the process. But can we say that none were created either?

The headline for Fiorina's letter was "Be Creative, Not Protectionist." The creativity in this case referred to the fact that we have to be creative as a society to reinvest in growth areas that create high-quality jobs and to take some responsibility for the people who are left jobless. This is just as it should be, as I advocated earlier.

Ms. Fiorina is obviously very sensitive to all the nuances of the situation and has all the right intentions. However, for all the wonderful words and good intentions, there is still the danger that outsourcing call center work can create a public relations nightmare. Even a thoughtful letter to the *Wall Street Journal* can be perceived as executive hand washing. So, all of you executives out there who are planning to outsource anything you can to reduce cost, take heed: Your reputation as a company is a very important part of your competitive advantage. Consumers and politicians are watching this trend to outsource very carefully, so you should behave like a responsible citizen, not like a reckless cost-cutting shark. Your goal is to cut costs *and* provide excellent customer service to your customers. Anything less would not be efficient.

There is some evidence, however, that sending jobs overseas adds jobs back home. Matthew Slaughter, an economist at Dartmouth College, pointed out in a *Wall Street Journal* editorial that analyzing outsourcing as a zero-sum game in which one job is substituted for another job ignores important factors. There are economic savings enjoyed by the company that does the outsourcing and by the consumer who purchases goods and service that are beneficial and may add jobs in the long term. Also, administrative work related to handling the offshore production requires a higher skill level than actually doing the production and so, arguably, adds jobs to the service sector (Slaughter 2004).

Whether we speak of the twentieth or twenty-first century, the industrialized world has endured many economic evolutions and revolutions. Again, outsourcing is not a new phenomenon. The transition from an agricultural to an industrial economy involved the displacement of all kinds of workers. The Luddites rioted against mechanization of the wool industry in Britain in the early 1800s. Large waves of immigrants from Europe to the United States in the late 1800s and early 1900s put tremendous downward pressure on service and factory wages. These trends are large and strong. They cannot be stopped, not completely, anyway. They can be tampered with through legislative action, one example of which is the Emergency Quota Act, created in 1921 to end mass immigration from Europe to the United States. History is full of similar legislative protections to preserve the status quo in the face of painful change. The future will no doubt prove the same.

2

The Customer Experience Dilemma

B efore delving into some of the more complex aspects of human interaction, let's agree that there are some universal things that customers want to see when calling for assistance with a problem. Several customer surveys, taken from around the world, consistently raise these same priorities. They may be in slightly different order, or one item may be missing because of the particular nature of that field, but the most surprising thing is the consistency with which people want to see answers to the following questions:

1. **Is anyone there?** The first thing we want to see is that someone picks up the phone. We can deal with a machine picking up the call if the machine provides logical options that actually lead us closer to a resolution. The perception of time is a huge cultural variable, but suffice it to say that no one anywhere enjoys hearing twenty rings before an answer or being put on hold for twenty minutes.
2. *Can* **you help me?** The second universal rule we will call *competence*. Here, we are simply dealing with the agent's ability to fix issues. Again, nobody anywhere enjoys dealing with untrained and unresponsive agents who don't know what they are talking about. Vendors and companies try to address this issue through various means, such as scripts, training, computer systems, and so forth.
3. **Are you courteous?** The third expectation of customers around the globe is some modicum of courtesy. Certainly there is some vari-

ance with regard to what is perceived as "courteous" behavior. Let us agree that most customers anywhere in the world want to have at least a civil exchange with a moderate amount of enthusiasm and simple courtesies such as *please* and *thank you.* There are some places, for example China and eastern Europe, where expectations regarding courtesy may be lower on the scale of priorities. Still, we would never set up a customer service operation and actually tell agents to treat customers harshly.

The three universal customer service qualities above are basic and fairly mechanical. There are many other categories that one could list when it comes to customer expectations, but upon close examination they generally fall as subsets of one of these three, excepting one—that more nebulous "customer experience." Customer experience is whatever you perceive it to be. On customer satisfaction surveys, *experience* is referred to as "know me/ know my business" empathy, enthusiasm, attitude, timing, and anything that conveys excellence or world-class attention to detail. We all have preferences, but our preferences may depend on the situation.

We may have particular criteria for vendors who provide services for us at work, and we may have another set of criteria for the phone company when we have to call and complain about the phone bill when we get home. Under these layers, we see that customer experience, more than any other factor, is culturally determined. Whereas an American customer might be very impressed with an agent who takes control of the situation and throws in a quick joke while the issue is being resolved, that behavior might be seen as disrespectful in other parts of the world. While a Japanese customer might be very satisfied with an agent who speaks softly in deference and respect, this tone might be interpreted as incompetence in other parts of the world. In order to examine our expectations and to try to pin down the concept of customer experience, let's explore it in the context of culture.

Culture and the Customer Experience

There are many long and boring definitions of culture, none of which will be repeated here. Edward T. Hall, a well-known anthropologist and author, offers a short but extremely powerful definition of culture that works well for the business environment in general and the call center in particular: *Culture is communication.* According to Hall, everything you do, every word you say, every expression you make—whether painting a portrait, building your first house, or even making a facial expression—is a reflection of your culture, your values, and beliefs as molded by your surroundings (Hall 1977).

We have already learned that customer experience is culturally determined. In other words, the way in which we perceive a customer experience is through the lenses of our own particular cultures. From a business perspective, it is vital that the service provider remember that the onus is on him to adapt to the culture of his customers. He cannot expect the customer to simply accept whatever level of service is provided. There are always alternative suppliers for the product or service that the customer is purchasing. A business cannot afford to rest on its laurels.

It's also true that for most people, we tend to want to communicate with others who communicate as we do. It is just easier that way. So, next we are going to learn more about communication *styles*—two core ones, high-context and low-context communication—which shed further light on the customer experience. Because we are using the definition of culture as communication, we are conveniently learning about culture at the same time.

High-Context Communication
Edward T. Hall also pioneered the terms *high context* and *low context* as a way to compare cultures. For the general business audience, Hall's definitions may be rather complex, but the knowledge and the lessons in his works are truly important for all of us. High-context communication refers to the fact that anything we say is composed of two things: *what* we say and *how* we say it. When we add the two together—*what* plus *how*—we arrive at the meaning behind what is being communicated. People from different cultures have a

tendency to vary the *what* and *how* that is encompassed in any given message. An illustration of high-context/low-context communication looks like this:

All communication is a mixture of high- and low-context content that represents one meaning in the encoder, and hopes to evoke a similar meaning in the decoder.

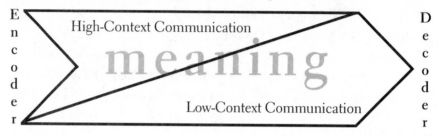

Adapted from Hall, 1977

The most important point of this illustration is that the meaning remains constant. In other words, people from different cultural groups have a need to convey the same messages. We just do so differently.

A high-context communication or message is one in which most of the information rests either in the physical context or is internalized by the communicating and receiving people alike, while very little is in the coded, explicit, transmitted part of the message. High-context communication may also rely to a greater extent on nonverbal communication, which takes many forms, including touch, gestures, physical appearance, posture, signs of comfort/tension, timing of responses, and facial expressions such as sadness and joy. It is implicit communication. It evokes shared experience with the other party. These expressions are culturally learned and can be difficult for outsiders to interpret. What they have in common is that they evoke the meaning in the other person.

It is common sense, then, that nonverbal communication tends to be particularly troublesome in a cross-cultural setting. Meanings differ from culture to culture. For example, a hand gesture has one very specific meaning in one culture and a completely different one in another culture. The protocol of conversation also differs greatly from culture to culture. In some cultures it is important—perhaps even critical—to make small talk first before moving on to business, while other cultures prefer to get right down to business. In some cultures it is polite to ask about family; in others that is not appropriate in a business setting. Think of it this way: If you are a nuclear physicist attending the annual meeting of nuclear physicists, you and your colleagues share the same context. You probably tell jokes that other people (perhaps even scientists from other specialties) would not understand. This is high-context communication. However, at the end of the convention when you have to issue a press release regarding your findings, you have to be very explicit about your findings to ensure that the outside community understands your research. Enter low-context communication.

Low-Context Communication

Low-context communication is just the opposite of high-context. In other words, the mass of the information is in the explicit code. Explicit code refers to language in the form of speech or writing. Language is reliable. Generally, there is agreement between speakers about words and their meanings, apart from those pesky idiomatic phrases. A good example of low context communication is a technical manual for consumer products, or at least it should be a good example if done properly. The communication that occurs in call centers is also, in most cases, low context. You want your agents to be explicit and consistent when they deliver messages. Of course, how they deliver the message is important as well—and the point behind this entire book. But getting the basic, explicit words across clearly is the prerequisite for everything else. I am not saying that this is easy, but it is something one should strive for on the call center floor in order to create an outstanding customer experience.

It's imperative that managers and trainers understand the difference between these two forms of communication and how they can subtly creep into conversations between customers and agents. For example, the professor in an introductory physics class would not talk to his class the same way he would talk to a convention of other physicists, would he? He would be much more explicit in the classroom to ensure that the students understood what he was trying to convey.

The Difference Between the Two

Years ago, while I was studying these basics of intercultural communication at the American University in Washington, D.C., my professor, Gary

Weaver, used this very effective anecdote to illustrate the difference between high- and low-context communication:

Remember back to the moment you first met your spouse or "significant other." In the beginning, you were getting to know each other. You asked a lot of questions. In doing so, you relied on an explicit exchange of words to get to know the other person. You were finding out if you were compatible. *This is low-context communication.*

As you got to know each other, your belief systems began to overlap because you were sharing experiences. And today you know the other person so well that you can communicate a lot of information using very few words. When you come home from a long day at the office, you might just throw your bag on the floor, plunk down in the most comfortable chair, and give a heavy sigh while covering your face with your hands. Your spouse or partner, in response, might give you a pat on the back and say: "Dinner will be ready in a few minutes." *You have just had a very high-context conversation.* You communicated a thousand words while uttering only a few, none of which related directly to what was said (Weaver 1988).

Now, ask yourself this: Could I have had that high-context exchange with some stranger off the street? Would he or she have understood what is going on at work right now, how I react to stressful situations, or what I need when I am tired? To some extent, maybe. But this conversation would not have been as satisfying. You would not be able to presume that the other person understood.

Although the previous example is drawn from personal life, the example still applies in a business setting where customer service agents are serving culturally diverse customers. There are many fine nuances as to how communication happens even in short and relatively trivial situations—even in call centers.

We can plot cultures along a continuum between lower context and higher context. Generally speaking, Western cultures are lower context and Eastern cultures are higher context, and when communication between the two groups occurs, you will quickly see how problems arise. When considering the concepts presented in the rest of this book, keep in mind that we were first defining communication style within cultures. Once we understand communication styles within cultures, we can move on to discussing communication between two or more different cultural groups (see Part II). For now, also understand that communicating through shared experience is more satisfying for all of us, including your customers.

Deny Thy Culture

As a businessperson, you may think we can just ignore that culture stuff. Cover up the accent and provide accurate scripts for the agent and everything will be fine. Especially in professional settings, we have tricked ourselves into thinking that we can present ourselves as we want others to see us or that we can train others to be as they are not. This is far from the truth. Most people can see straight through us. The reason is that most of what we communicate to the rest of the world is nonverbal. What is more, it is nearly impossible to hide those nonverbal signals.

Sure, it is easier to control what we say explicitly. But, in learning theory, it is well known that hearing for only accounts about 11 percent of learning. Sight, on the other hand, accounts for over 80 percent of what a person learns. From an evolutionary point of view, anthropologists know that at some point humans began to rely more on sight and less on smell.

Why is it impossible to disguise nonverbal cues? It is because most of the values and beliefs that we reflect nonverbally are held very deeply. So deeply, in fact, we are not conscious of them. These are often things we learned in our youth from our parents and that are deeply ingrained. We learn fundamental things such as definitions of what is beautiful and what is ugly. We learn the fine nuances of socially acceptable behavior. We learn posture, timing, and concepts of good and evil. Once those building blocks are all in place, they become very difficult to move or change in any way. Think of them as a pyramid built of blocks of values. In our daily lives, we judge the world around us through the context of those values. It happens every minute of every day and night, even in our dreams. Note that I use *beliefs* and *values* interchangeably here. *Beliefs* relate to that which we deem to be true or not true, whereas *values* relate to what we judge as good or bad. For our purposes here, they serve the same function. They constitute the scales of measurement to evaluate events and situations as we encounter them.

Many cross-cultural experts such as Hall use a Freudian interpretation to explain belief systems. I don't know how many times I have heard belief systems likened to an iceberg. The idea is that most of what we believe is below the surface, where we cannot see it. It is unconscious (Hall 1977). I do not subscribe to this metaphor, not because it is untrue or erroneous, but because it somehow gets interpreted as an excuse for ignorance. In our heads we say, "Oh, that belief stuff is unconscious so I can't really affect that." Not exactly. It is all there to be seen if you are willing to take the time to really focus on it. The fact that most of us do not do this kind of self-reflection on an ongoing basis is a different issue altogether. You and your agents' cultures are there to be seen by all, including you.

Achieving Integrity with Nonverbal Communication

Have you ever known someone to say one thing and feel another? The truth will shine through every time. The obvious example of incongruent customer service is the flight attendant who has been serving drinks and cleaning up after cranky customers during an eight-hour flight, yet he stands at the exit door smiling, saying "Bye-bye, hope to see you again soon" to every single customer stepping off the plane. Everyone who looks at him knows he has had enough. He just wants to go back to the hotel and take his shoes off. Yet, he stands there, smiling, saying it. Why? It is almost tragic. Maybe that is why comedians have had so much fun with the exit-the-plane-bye-bye-scene. If I were an airline advisor, I would recommend a nonsmiling, sincere "thank you" instead.

There is a huge variable in nonverbal communication that is particularly relevant to call center interaction called *integrity*. Nonverbal communication includes tone of voice, conversational cadence and pace, intonation, facial expression, gestures, spatial arrangements, eye contact, patterns of touch, and expressive movement: cues that are outside the realm of the language itself. It relates to the urgency with which we say something. We can come across as rushed, apologetic, submissive, dominant, harsh, careless, pleasant, fun, foolish, dry, tender, approachable, remote, nervous, eager to please, detached, engaged, serious, and myriad other traits—all conveyed nonverbally. Integrity is the congruity between the intended and the actual. Having integrity means being who you really are. In short, it is consistency between saying and doing. And it is a prerequisite for creating the intended effect in customer service settings. Only integrity can evoke the right emotion.

Customers want to have an experience on to their own terms, their own culturally determined terms, that is. They want the expected response, the norm. But, what is normal? Normal things are things that we are used to seeing all the time. Dealing with things that are different from what you know or see as "normal" can be difficult. When we are presented with a concept or idea that conflicts with our pyramid of values, we have two options: we can either reject it completely as false, or we can rearrange our belief system to make room for the new concept. This rearranging process is painful, so the tendency is to reject new ideas. You can test yourself if you think about a controversial topic that you feel strongly about such as abortion or gun control. Just think of the rearranging that you would have to do to your value system to change your mind on one of those topics. The very same principle operates on a much more subtle level even in customer service situations. You can notice the rejection in yourself when you get an unexpected, in your eyes unsuitable, customer service response. There is an instant negativity. You cover it up, but you have dismissed the other person's behavior as wrong.

From a customer's perspective, we want an interaction that is consistent with our expectations. It means the agent is expected to empathize with the customer and provide a culture-appropriate response. An agent who does not understand the customer's culture and point of view may have the best of intentions yet still behave incongruently, seeming to lack integrity to the customer. In my opinion, this is the main problem in locating call centers on the other side of the world. Part of it relates to the agent and how he reacts to situations from moment to moment. There is no hiding of nonverbal cues. People are sponges when it comes to nonverbal communication. We often misinterpret, but we absorb it, nevertheless. The other problem relates to the training the agent receives. Scripted responses do a tremendous amount of damage to the customer-perceived integrity of the agent. Once the agent has lost integrity in the eyes of the customer, it is all over. There is no repairing that relationship in the short time frame that we are talking about. Do you want support and advice from someone whom you have no confidence in? Lack of integrity is a deep flaw in any culture. No culture embraces a liar or regards deceit as a virtue.

The Silent Causes of Miscommunication

All these nonverbal cues and values cause misunderstanding and miscommunication in the call center. I have tried to divide the most frequently encountered of these problems into three easy-to-understand categories: time, "comparisms," and rules. This format provides a useful framework for alerting agents to anticipate how misunderstandings can occur.

Time

In 2002, DirectTV's customer service operations were ranked number one in the cable- and satellite-TV industry by J. D. Power & Associates, the American Customer Satisfaction Index, and the Yankee Group. This is obviously not a small achievement. Over the course of two years, DirectTV increased the percentage of customers who ranked their service as satisfactory from 80 percent to 93 percent. This increase was accomplished through a series of steps to improve employee morale, motivation, and empowerment to make decisions. However, there is one fundamental change that probably contributed to the transformation more than anything else. DirectTV dropped agent evaluation based on talk-time, giving the agents the freedom to handle each call with the necessary courtesy and attention to detail. For those who are new to call center terminology, *talk-time* is the time the agent spends on the phone handling the issue (Parks 2003).

Often, agents are restricted in terms of the amount of time they are allowed to use to resolve issues. One employee who quit in 2000 summed up his experience as follows: "My good deeds never went unpunished. It did not matter if I sold the best packages all day. If they wanted my talk-time to be eight minutes and it took me ten, I knew I would get someone stopping by my desk." Everyone knows that it is much less expensive to retain an existing customer than it is to acquire a new one. The new, unlimiting time-talk strategy adds cost to DirectTV's customer support, but that cost has to be weighed against the benefit of acquiring new customers.

This example is particularly remarkable because it is an intra-American operation. Americans and northern Europeans have a concept of time that is very different from most of the rest of the world. Time is perhaps the topic with the greatest potential to make or break cross-border call center interactions. Time management is your best friend and your worst enemy, a double-edged sword either to be restricted to reduce cost, or to be allotted generously to allow agents to provide excellent customer service.

Call centers, for the most part, were invented and are still mostly conceived and implemented by Westerners. In the call center universe, time is money. The term "agent utilization" oozes with economic theory of how to make lots and lots of money. A call center manager's day is mostly a matter of servicing the maximum number of calls using just the right-sized staff.

In the West, time is rigid and linear. Time is a tangible, quantifiable commodity that can be bought, sold, given, borrowed, lent, saved, and wasted. In non-Western cultures, time is fluid and flexible. It is relative. If you, the reader, learn nothing else by reading this book, learn this:

In non-Western cultures relationships *take precedence over* tasks.

Relationships, including casual call center interactions, are part of the realm of being. In non-Western cultures, *being* is more important than *doing*. That is why, as you will see in later discussion, attentive listening that allows the customer to take his time to fully complete his or her thought process is stressed when training agents who deal with non-Western customers. *Allowing the pause* and *being with the moment* are concepts that are sometimes hard for Western agents to learn, yet they are a vital part of non-Western culture.

Tasks are part of the realm of time—wrap up the call in three minutes, answer the call within thirty seconds, the meeting starts at nine, finish this report by noon, and so on. In the West, we are what we do and doing things takes time, so you have to use your time efficiently. Our entire school systems are rigorously designed to enforce this efficiency as a primary value. Little Johnny should not play too long with the other children, because then he will not finish his homework. And if he does not finish his homework, he will not get a good grade. And if he does not get a good grade, he will not get into medical school.

The DirectTV example is not an anomaly. As we have learned, there are variations and exceptions in people's values and perceptions within every culture. Agents are smart. If trained on the concept of time, they can assess whether the customer is in a hurry and wants to wrap up the transaction quickly. They can also sense if someone wants to have a more complete interaction and adjust accordingly.

"Comparisms"

I have lumped a number of cultural traits together into one overall group that I call "comparisms." Every one of these traits creates a perceived qualitative difference between you and the other person, that is very different from time perceptions and the next category, rules. Gender, age, face, and belonging can all cause the customer to ascribe to you, the agent, a certain status.

Gender. Customers may have a preference for women or men on an individual basis when it comes to customer service. In some cultures, males may be uncomfortable with women providing the customer service. This could be because women are seen as being of a lower status than males or because of traditional gender roles. Middle Eastern cultures tend to see women more in traditional roles than in professional settings, but it is dangerous to make such generalizations. The bottom line is that gender could cause miscommunication or discomfort, and if you sense that this is happening, the best option is probably to try to accommodate the customer. Explain to agents that they are in no position to change anyone's values during a brief interaction, whether the customer is right or wrong.

Age. Many cultures ascribe higher status to older members of society. That means that there may be cases when an older person feels uncomfortable receiving instructions and help from a younger person. On a day-to-day basis this may be difficult to control. However, if you have an important customer from Japan, let's say, and you need to assign an agent to handle that customer's issues on an ongoing basis, you then have an opportunity to offer experience and make your customer feel more comfortable.

Take a look at the following training activity for an example of how age and gender could impact a customer service call.

 TRAINING ACTIVITY: Gender and Status

Ask two people to act out the following scenario: A bank in London has recently landed a new customer in Dubai. It is a very large account, so the ACD has been configured to route calls from this account to the most senior agent available. Today, the most senior agent available is Ms Speakwell. She is a young star in the call center. She sees on her screen that the new account in Dubai is on the line, sits up straight, and answers the phone in her signature, friendly greeting:

> Ms. Speakwell: "Good morning, London Commerce Bank, Ms. Speakwell speaking, how may I help you?"
>
> Mr. Sharif: (Long pause.) "Good morning, Ms. Speakwell. How are you today?"
>
> Ms. Speakwell: I am very well, thank you, how may I help you today?
>
> Mr. Sharif: "I have an important matter. May I please speak with your manager?"
>
> Ms. Speakwell: "Certainly, sir. However, it appears Mrs. Knowall is on another line at this time. I should be able to handle most any issue, however.
>
> Mr. Sharif: Is there another manager I can speak with?
>
> Ms. Speakwell: Sorry, sir. Mrs. Knowall is the manager on duty. Can I put you on hold or put you through to her voice mail?"
>
> Mr. Sharif: (Pause.) "I will call back at another time, thank you."
>
> Ms. Speakwell: "Very well, Mr. Sharif, thank you for calling London Commerce Bank."
>
> Mr. Sharif: "Good-bye."
>
> Ms. Speakwell: "Good-bye."

Ask the participants what they think happened during the interaction. Mr. Sharif wanted to speak with someone who was more on his level, organizationally. This is common in many non-Western countries. Further, he would rather speak with a man regarding important issues. This is common in Middle Eastern cultures, particularly traditional Muslim cultures. Explain that agents should not take this personally. When faced with either talking to Ms. Speakwell or leaving a message for Mrs. Knowall, Mr. Sharif felt he had no options left but to call again at another time. The best action would have been to pass the call to another senior male agent.

Face. "Face" is a phenomenon that really has no comparable expression in Western culture. It is a "comparism" because it points to an individual's perception of how the rest of the world views him—with honor or dishonor. From that perspective, very subtle behaviors can cause you to inadvertently disrespect someone, causing them to lose face. Face influences a large part of feelings and behavior for most of the population of the world, including most Latin, African, Asian, and Middle Eastern cultures.

For me, understanding the concept of face has been slow in coming. At first, it seemed alien and even silly to me. At some point I understood. I don't know exactly when. It is real and tangible to the many other cultures. Just as time is a tangible for me in the West, face is a tangible thing in high-context cultures. It is like a barometer that constantly measures your honor as you interact with the people around you. It relates directly to what they mostly identify with—who you are, *being*—just as time is intricately bound to our Western identity of *doing*.

If an agent calls a senior manager in Japan and does not use the proper title to address him or jumps right into conversation without any courtesies, he or she could cause the Japanese manager's face barometer to go down dramatically. The agent and the company (which, by the way, are one and the same for the Japanese manager) have not fully understood who he is, a person of status who deserves to be treated as such.

The most important thing to remember is to allow your agents to perform common courtesies in greeting customers thoroughly. Take the customer's lead with regard to small talk before and during business talk. This can be done by allowing for pauses in the conversation. These pauses are not perceived as uncomfortable silence as we in the West might perceive them. Instead they are seen as a courtesy. You are pausing to ensure that the person has fully completed his thoughts. As easy as this might sound, it is a fine art that comes only with experience.

 ## TRAINING ACTIVITY: Yes, No, and the Importance of Face

Here is an example of how face can enter into call center communications: An American software company has distributed a beta version of a new application to a small set of user groups around the world. An agent has been assigned to call one individual per user group to get early feedback and initial impressions. The application is completely out of step with what people in the field need. It uses the wrong technology and approaches to solve the issues. Listen to how each beta user is attempting to convey this same message to John in San Jose:

> Agent John in San Jose: Please give us some observations on how this application might help you solve your problems.
>
> Olaf in Norway: This will not work at all. You are using a locally installed application when we need a web-based architecture to address our warehouse integration.
>
> Hiro in Tokyo: Hhhssss [sucking in air through his teeth to express discomfort]. Yes, hello, John. Very nice to speak to you. We have also seen a competitor's solution that uses a distributed platform. That was very nice for warehouse integration.
>
> Raj in Bombay: Yes, I see. Very nice. You have some very good programmers there in San Jose [spoken enthusiastically]. With respect, sir, this may have to be modified [his tone dropping to express discomfort at having to deliver bad news]. Have you considered how our distributed warehouses might be integrated using this solution?

Despite the differences in their words, each of these beta testers is far from pleased with the product. Think about this situation for a moment, because this is simple, yet powerful. Note in particular how the beta users in Tokyo and Bombay are both prompting John to come to his own realization that this application is a disaster. Saying so directly would cause John to lose face, so they will avoid this at all cost. But they are still being honest in their opinions. If John in San Jose does not know what to listen for, he may return a scorecard that says the application is seen as favorable by 60 percent of the beta testers. If John knows what to listen for, he can tell his bosses that they need to start from scratch.

Belonging. In the West, people identify with what they *do*, their occupation. Many non-Westerners identify more strongly with their group, their family, or their village. Those things are who they *are*. This difference creates some very interesting differences in how a person feels when things go wrong during an interaction. Because people are individualistic in the West, if they fail to get something done or if we do something wrong, the individual feels guilt. You have failed yourself and everything that you stand for. On a deeper level this could even be guilty before God. What happened violated your belief system. For group-oriented, non-Western cultures, transgression still causes shame, but for different reasons. You feel you have let down the group around you. They share your shame.

Understanding how people derive identity enables the agent to provide effective flattery. A mobile phone service agent dealing with a Westerner might say, "I see you have made an excellent choice in selecting this phone. It is one of the best available." Selecting the phone was a *do*. Doing something well builds identity in the Western mind-set. The agent has shown respect for the customer's abilities. The same agent dealing with someone from Mexico might do better in saying, "My sister came back from vacation in Mexico last week. She said it was the most beautiful country she has ever seen." Being Mexican is a strong factor in how the Mexican customer derives his identity. It is part of what he *is*. The agent has just complimented the customer's homeland and by doing so strengthened the relationship.

Many non-Western cultures place a lot of emphasis on where you are from and where you belong. India's caste system is probably the most obvious example of this phenomenon, but it can be found in many, many other countries as well. In Greece and Mexico, there is a strong awareness of what village or town you are from. People can identify you quickly by the way you talk and by the way you look.

Volumes can be written about how to deal with this attitude in interpersonal settings. When it comes to call center operations, the consequences of labelling or having been labeled are very different from situation to situation. The basic question to ask is, how will the customer react when she reaches the person in customer support? The classic example of dealing with this issue is the decision to put a center in the mid-western part of the United States when serving North American customers, because the American Midwest accent tends to be perceived as neutral by most North Americans.

In non-Western cultures it is often more important to have acceptance from your group than to earn individual achievement. The issue of group acceptance can cause problems in call center settings. Let's say an agent is handling a complex issue and is requesting that the customer provide an answer or a decision regarding the issue. A person from Mexico or Japan, both high-context cultures where the at-large group plays an important role in daily life, may find it very uncomfortable to provide an answer without first consulting with the group. This will depend on the situation, but for the high-context individual, to give the wrong answer can have serious consequences later, causing group rejection and loss of face. If the low-context agent pressures the customer for information because of time, the customer may literally shut down. The group is much more important than any individual case or issue. It would be better to let it go than disappoint the group.

Rules

In the West, people believe what they can see. Western countries have elaborate legal systems with overt, documented rules. Put it in writing, they say. Talk is cheap. Rules are explicit, written down in law books and spelled out in processes and procedures. The rules in your call center are likely spelled out clearly for all to see. Individuals are comfortable with rules and derive a sense of comfort from the fact that everyone is following them.

In high-context cultures, the individual depends on the group for support, and the group depends on the individual. Part of this group dynamic are implicit rules of behavior. In Mexican culture, written rules exist in relative importance to implicit, unwritten rules. Everyone is aware that in order to move the legal system, one has to pay a little money. It is called *la mordida*, literally meaning *the bite*. An officer of the law will simply be a little uncooperative until he is paid a nominal amount. This tradition is not written down anywhere, but everyone knows about it. It is implied.

The most common way that this implicit kind of rule can affect call center interaction is that a non-Westerner is more comfortable with accepting that there is more than one way to resolve an issue while a Westerner is likely to feel best when the rule book is followed strictly. Let your agents know that if they have problems doing things exactly by the book with a non-Westerner, they should provide the person on the other end with additional context about why it is important to follow the rules. Let's say rule 132-B states, that clients cannot hold money in temporary escrow accounts for more than fifteen days. A client from Mexico is insisting that they need to hold the money there for thirty days. Instead of saying "rule number 132-B states . . . ," the agent could say something to the effect that "in our experience, doing things the following way results in better outcomes because . . ."

In many non-Western cultures, things don't exist in a vacuum—all things are related, and this affects the perspective on rules. Medicine is an excellent example of holistic versus particulate perspectives. In Western medicine we have one kind of doctor for each body part and function. Compare this approach to Chinese medicine, which sees the body and spirit as a whole with approach a cause and effect between the two.

The agent may see examples of this difference when a non-Western customer describes a problem, giving plenty of additional context in describing an issue. Further, the agent is now part of the issue, and the customer may feel a need to engage the agent deeply and personally in resolving it. In contrast, a Swede or a German would be fine with solving only the specific problem at hand. The best coping strategy is for agents to allow themselves to become personally involved in issues on an anecdotal level. They can play along and empathize in the scenarios provided by the customer. Should the personal involvement reach inappropriate levels, the agent should provide context as to why something is unacceptable rather than abruptly break the flow of the conversation.

Conflict and How We Deal with It

Geert Hofstede, another pioneer in intercultural communication, is a Dutch scholar and author who classified cultures along four dimensions: masculinity/femininity, individualism/collectivism, uncertainty avoidance, and power distance (Hofstede 1997). Individualism/collectivism is much like the group dynamics described earlier. Uncertainty avoidance has many exceptions, so it will not be dealt with here. The other two dimensions, however, masculinity/femininity and power distance, are very powerful concepts in the call center setting.

Feminine versus Masculine Cultures

Feminine cultures tend to be more nurturing. The most feminine cultures on Hofstede's scale are Scandinavian countries and the Netherlands. The extensive welfare systems in those countries are examples of how that feminine nature manifests itself. Justice is also handed down gently, with shorter sentencing and many rehabilitation services.

Masculine countries, such as Japan, Austria, and to some extent the United States, tend to be ones in which assertiveness, aggressiveness, and competition take center stage. Individuals in masculine countries tend to be more comfortable with settling issues through a healthy debate. Great Britain is a prime example of a masculine country. The interaction in the British House of Commons shows how this can be both constructive and entertaining. It does, however, cause serious problems when one takes this approach with a person from a feminine culture. Feminine cultures generally resolve issues through consensus, whereas this drawn-out process makes people from masculine counties become impatient. A person from a feminine culture is more likely to balk at and withdraw from conflict.

I want to provide an anecdote to illustrate how this difference in approach to conflict resolution can surface in the call center. As a preface, please be aware that there are many nuances to this story, meaning it cannot be interpreted simply in terms of feminine versus masculine traits. The example involves a technology company that had agents in North America and Europe. Their role was to work complex technical tickets, fixing problems around the world. These technical problems could be very serious, with multimillion dollar accounts on the line. In other words, the situations were often urgent. As this urgency was experienced by the U.S. agents, naturally, it was impossible to conceal. In passing the tickets, the Americans sounded rushed and maybe even a little pushy. Agents in Europe consistently told me the same things: "Those Americans are so rude. Do they think we are stupid?" In particular, agents in the Netherlands and Dutch speakers in Belgium, both feminine groups, would complain, neatly illustrating the Hofstede dimension. But agents in the United Kingdom and Germany were uncomfortable with the communication style of these Americans as well. Those are both cultures that rank as very masculine, so why did they not just push back and indulge the Americans in a healthy discussion? Consistently, the sense of urgency that was conveyed by using what was perceived as rudeness actually slowed things down, a passive-aggressive reaction perhaps.

As I said, there are other cultural variations at work here. The U.K. agents, for example, would not react angrily in return. Better to respond with an ironic quip to show control over the situation. As for the Germans, I suspect language has something to do with the reason they did not push back. They were native Germans working in an English-speaking environment. Those of you who have learned a second language know that engaging in an emotional argument in that language is very difficult. The necessary vocabulary is just not there, and when in an emotional state, one simply can't retrieve the words fast enough. Also, the Germans probably already felt very committed to resolving things as quickly as possible. In Germany, one would trust that all those around you have the same level of commitment to the work. There is no need to reinforce it with emotional urgency. Germans take a procedural approach. If everyone knows the procedures, there is no need to remind colleagues about why or how soon things should be tended to.

There is another theme in this story, and it relates to perceptions of time. This topic is discussed under a separate heading, but I find it intriguing that Germany, Japan, the United Kingdom and the United States are all generally masculine cultures that are also very punctual, yet each tends to react differently when that time sensitivity creates a pressure-filled situation. Below are some recommendations for diffusing pressure-filled situations with masculine cultures. While you read, imagine that each person is experiencing the same sense of stress due to some critical deadline approaching. The reactions that time pressures evoke are culturally recognizable.

- As an American gets flustered and rushed, empathize with him. You can do this by conveying the same sense of urgency. This approach will make the American feel that he has an ally, and it can diffuse some of the pressure.
- The Englishman is more likely to appear very cool and calm. He may even exaggerate the sense of calm for comedic effect. I suggest you join in for a moment and then calmly start talking about the details that need to be attended to. Be very careful not to condescend. You are very likely not dealing with a dummy, so give the benefit of the doubt. Agree to follow up shortly to ensure closure on the issue. This reaction helps assure him that you are equally involved in and attentive to the problem.
- As for the German and Japanese participants, my sense is that the likelihood of either of them resorting to pushy or rude behavior will depend a lot on the context of the situation. Rank will certainly play a role in how they react. For both groups, how close you are to the situation, meaning whether you are a close colleague or a stranger, will also influence the reaction more significantly than it will with the American or the Englishman. If things have escalated to emotional reactions, you may want to show some level of guilt to the German and shame to the Japanese person in order to diffuse the situation and then appeal for a more procedural way toward resolution.

Power Distance

Power distance determines how we relate to authority as individuals. It also determines how steeply organizations tend to organize themselves; in other words, are they "flat" or hierarchical in nature? Countries with low-power distance include Scandinavian countries and the Netherlands. The United States has relatively low-power distance as well. High- power distance can be found in France, Germany, and many Asian countries. For a person from a high-power distance country, it may be important to talk only to someone of equal rank. They may ask to speak with a manager even though nothing has gone wrong. Should this happen, train your agents not to take this personally.

Agents in high-power distance cultures will also have a lower comfort level when it comes to taking independent initiatives or being asked to come up with creative solutions on the fly. The relationship between manager and subordinate is one in which the subordinate depends on the manager for direction and guidance. These agents literally want clear instructions and parameters within which to operate. Requesting them to think out of the box can cause extreme anxiety much in the same way that a person from a low-power distance culture would feel stifled by excessive rules and regiments with no empowerment to improve and improvise.

People in high-power distance cultures are less likely to want to challenge authority. You should find out how your customers perceive your company when they call you. Are they calling down to a support person who is beneath them, or are they calling up to an authority in the industry or the community? For example, your attitude is going to be very different when you call the Internal Revenue Service about your taxes as opposed to calling Best Buy because they are late in returning a $5 refund.

Please know that my goal in this chapter is not to resolve the issue of customer experience for you. I cannot give a few bullets on this or that culture to an agent and expect him or her to create a perfect customer experience. This chapter is merely intended to create a framework and develop some level of appreciation for how difficult it is to achieve satisfactory customer experience across cultures. An opportunity to create optimal experience will only come with more immersion into the belief system of the customer's culture. Immersion could mean anything from a day of focused training to a month of in-country training. In the end, it is my hope that you will be motivated to learn far more than this book can offer about the culture of your customers and how it relates to how they perceive you.

3

Understanding the Media of Interaction

When communication breaks down, the problem occurs in the decoding of the message (Weaver 1988). The sender usually has every intention of expressing himself clearly, but it is in the receiving of the message that the problem occurs. The following example illustrates several aspects of how nonverbal cues—again, vocal and other cues outside of language and words—get misinterpreted in a face-to-face conversation.

An Afghan friend of mine is at a train station in Germany. He is a sophisticated man who speaks four languages, has impeccable manners, always wears good suits, and is well traveled. He walks up to the information booth to get instructions on how to get to the next train. He explains to the young German woman in the information booth that he needs to go to Vienna. She tells him what he needs to do. He does not understand. She tells him again. He still does not understand and requests that she explain again. This time, the woman at the information booth is visibly irritated. She raises her voice and provides the instructions in a manner that clearly lets my friend know that he is less than intelligent. My friend does not react to her outburst. He points to the queue behind him, which is quite long, and says, "Do not be upset with me. I am not your problem. You see all these nice people here. That is your problem."

This is a true story of what happens every day around the globe as people who are culturally different interact. What happened during this exchange? Who got upset first? The woman in the information booth got upset because she was not understood. Not being understood is very frustrating for humans (more about this topic in the next chapter). Of course, in a customer service exchange, not getting the information you need can be frustrating as well. My Afghan friend knew he was going to get to his train one way or another. As an Afghan, he was mostly concerned with having a cordial exchange with the other person, ensuring that their sense of honor and respect remained intact. The German woman in the information booth was probably very concerned with time in that situation, as punctuality is important in most Western cultures, and she was indeed concerned with the length of the queue.

In this example, the Afghan man, despite his sophistication, sent out a million signals that were a reflection of his culture. He probably stood close to the woman in the booth. He probably smiled and inserted as many niceties as he could into the conversation. The German woman, on the other hand, was probably serious. She was likely tense to begin with because the line was long. Her eyes were wandering from the clock to the queue to the customer. As we discussed in the first chapter, time and task are so intertwined that they are really two sides of the same coin. Anyone who has been to Germany knows that time is a core theme in German culture. Punctuality is very important. For Afghans, relationships are more important than anything. Strangers must be treated with the utmost courtesy. When we communicate, we expect people to pick up on our cues. However, when we communicate across cultures, the cues get lost. They are misinterpreted. They can distract, confuse, or, at worst, they can offend.

The Limits of Telephone Interaction

Knowing that most of what we communicate is nonverbal, it is easy to see that a large amount of context is missing when we interact over the telephone. Eye contact, or lack thereof, is a huge variable in establishing rapport with another person. One might argue that this reduction of non-verbal communication over the telephone reduces the opportunities for misunderstanding. That is not to say, however, that there is necessarily an improved opportunity for good communication. This will likely vary from situation to situation. While we are speaking of contact, it is interesting to note that eye contact protocol varies from culture to culture. For example, in some Asian cultures looking down is a sign of respect, whereas doing so can be interpreted as hesitation or a lack of confidence in Western cultures. Americans maintain eye contact about 80 to 90 percent of the time during a conversation. Anything less would be interpreted as either dishonesty or disinterest.

It is important to remember the nonverbal cues that are still there during voice-only conversations. Agents are always trained to "put a smile" in their voice, and it is true that cadence and intonations of a positive nature carry across wires and across cultures. Smiles are not interpreted the same way from culture to culture, however. I have seen training programs emphasizing that "a smile is always a smile in every language." Not true. Americans, and American women in particular, have been raised to smile incessantly in any given situation. Unfortunately, this habit is often interpreted as insincerity, particularly by many Europeans. The excessive enthusiasm seems completely out of context for most customer service situations. A German, for instance, would probably rather deal with a calm and competent agent than a bubbly one.

In general, I would advocate that agents take a more neutral outlook when handling calls. By neutral, I mean that one should not try to have an agenda during the call. When we adopt a more neutral position, particularly in cross-cultural situations, we also reduce the amount of context being transmitted: cheerfulness, persuasiveness, seriousness, urgency, or any other nonverbal voice position. Those voice positions have a great opportunity to be misinterpreted by the person on the other end of the line. (More detail about this neutral position can be found in Part II.)

 ## TRAINING ACTIVITY: Perceptions

Ask agents to talk about how and why emotional positions such as cheerfulness, persuasiveness, seriousness, or urgency might be problematic in cross-cultural situations. Have them work from their personal experiences and construct scenarios to illustrate what they predict might occur. Then have them refer to Part III to see if their perceptions are matched by this author's research and to explore the probable reactions to the same scenarios if the participants had been from other cultures.

The Ability to Speak Clearly

The safest bet is always going to be to let customers speak to agents who are similar to themselves. This creates the best opportunity for a positive inter-action. How often have you received a telephone solicitation from someone who can't pronounce your name, has an accent that is so strong that you can barely understand what he is saying, and possesses a conversational pro-tocol that is completely alien to you. It clearly does not produce results. That agent's job is to speak, and if he can't speak in a manner that allows you to understand him, then why is he even calling?

I know a call center training manager who makes his new hires read Shakespeare on the first day of induction training. If they can't speak clearly, they are not invited back for the second day of training. The ability to form complete sentences is not a birthright anywhere. Surveys of cus-tomers regarding speech indicate that one of the most irritating speech de-fects is mumbling. Think about it. Mumbling is annoying. When we hear mumbling, most of us wince in pain and ask "What?" Mumbling is strange that way. We want to understand, and when we can't, we instinctively blame the other person for not making himself clear.

The Importance of Reflective Listening

While there are entire books and training courses on the topic of reflective listening, the key points bear repeating here in the context of cross-cultural customer service. Reflective listening is the practice of simply repeating back to the customer what was just said in an effort to ensure everything was understood correctly. Most good agent training classes include reflective lis-tening skills. Every agent should know that repeating back what a customer from a different culture has said is a very powerful way to ensure that you understand each other. Simple concepts are often the most powerful ones, so let's take a closer look at how this works.

 TRAINING ACTIVITY: Reflective Listening

Have the agents repeat the following sentences and scenarios and discuss how they feel after each one. Have them assume the sentence is wrong. What does the customer have to do to reverse the statement under each scenario?

Scenario 1, reflective listening with a close-ended question
"So, per your request, I will transfer $50,000 from your account in Hong Kong to your account in Tokyo and put a hold on your futures call in New York. Is there anything else I can do for you today?"

Scenario 2, reflective listening with a pause for verification
"So, per your request, I will transfer $50,000 from your account in Hong Kong to your account in Tokyo and put a hold on your futures call in New York." (Pause, wait for customer response)

Often, we follow our reflective listening statements with a close-ended question such as "Did I understand you correctly?" The answer to that question is either a yes or a no. This is a problematic area in cross-cultural customer service. In many "face cultures," your customer is not going to want to reply no to such a question for fear it will cause you to lose face.

Adding a phrase like, "Is there anything else that I can help you with today?" can also create problems, since it creates a perception that whatever preceded it was true. It is tantamount to saying, "Now that we are done with this, can we move on to that?" If the customer disagrees with the first statement, he is forced to completely start from scratch.

Usually, it is enough to simply avoid closed-ended questions. In a banking situation, the agent might say something like this: "So, per your request, I will transfer $50,000 from your account in Hong Kong to your account in

Tokyo and put a hold on your futures call in New York." This is followed by a pause that will allow the customer to take corrective action, if necessary, without insulting you. Less is more. Allow a pause so the customer can contemplate for a moment what to say next. Close-ended questions are often filler phrases that Westerners like to throw in because they get uncomfortable with even a small moment of silence.

It should also be said that there is a danger of overdoing reflective listening. All that repetition takes time, and to the customer who does not need everything repeated back, it can actually be annoying. The key for the agent is to know when repeating things back is necessary and when it is not. Rookie agents often use reflective listening as a way to check if they are doing what the customer wants them to do. In other words, there is an ironic twist in roles, in which the agent is looking to the customer to drive the conversation. Experienced agents know what customers need before they even know it themselves. Those kinds of agents are more like situational therapists who guide customers to realize what they want—the polar opposite of robotically repeating back what the customer has said. Which kind of customer service would you rather have?

Purely from the perspective of having a positive interpersonal experience, a same-culture high-context interaction is generally the most satisfying. But it is precisely because this situation is impossible in a cross-cultural setting that we have to rely on things such as reflective listening to ensure we understand each other correctly. Put another way, adding extra context artificially takes some of the fun out of the exchange. However, that is a small price to pay for the alternative, which is miscommunication and its consequences.

Written Communication: Avoiding the Service Call

Up to this point, we have assumed that the communication between you and your customers takes place over the telephone. There are many other ways to interact with the customer, however. The first time may be when the customer sees your product on the shelf in the store, on your Web site, or in marketing literature. Those messages are usually carefully crafted.

Marketing professionals are usually well aware of the obstacles in overcoming cultural nuances. Most consumer companies simply arrange for a local marketing company to craft a campaign, because consumers in different cultures have markedly different values regarding what is a good product and what they can live without. For instance, the stereotype is that Germans like to be presented with scientific facts. Their car ads will include a lot of data indicating quality and performance. Consumers in the United Kingdom tend to like humor, while French consumers are wowed through style and wit. While it would be easy to find examples to reinforce these stereotypes on any given day in any given media format, it would be equally easy to locate exceptions. The best resource for marketing and branding of your products, therefore, is local marketing talent.

The second time you interact with the consumer is after the consumer has bought your product, taken it home, and is reading the technical manual. It impossible to estimate how many calls to customer service centers are due to inadequate, badly written manuals. Suffice it to say that most of us have been in that situation. I have bought products with manuals that have clearly not been written by native English speakers, which only creates an increasing volume of calls to contend with. Remember, call centers are cost centers. The goal is to reduce the number of calls you get from your customers. Nothing will reduce your call volume like having good documentation. Good documentation needs to be part of the entire company culture. If a company is willing to pass on bad documentation to customers, what will agents have to work with in terms of product information and job aids? The agent's written tools are not likely to be any better than what the customer has, so their ability to improve your situation is hampered from the outset.

Good documentation has the following characteristics:

- It is originally written by a person who is closely familiar with the product.
- It is written by someone with strong skills in technical writing (no matter what the language).
- It has been thoroughly reviewed and tested, anticipating customer questions.

- It is translated by native speakers into the local language where the product will be sold.
- After translation, it is reviewed again by other native speakers to ensure that it is accurate.

At this point, let us take a few steps back and observe what we are doing from a macro-perspective, remembering the basic premise of this book: People in different cultures communicate with one other differently, and when people from different cultures interact, there are often misunderstandings. Clearly, this is something we want to avoid. Technical documentation is the lowest-context form of communication, but when well-written it does a beautiful job of providing clear answers to anybody, anywhere.

Low- and High-Context Written Communication

Returning once again to the definitions of low and high context, is there such a thing as high-context written communication? Absolutely. It is called poetry. Poetry evokes common experience in much the same way as other forms of high-context communication described previously in the book do.

Here is an example of low context versus high context written directions:

High Context

The place where you need to go is across the river, just past the old oak tree, in the house where the miller used to live.

Low Context

1. Take Route 7 north.
2. Just past the river, turn left on Eighth Street (there will be a large oak tree on your right).
3. 1234 Eighth Street is the third house on the left (there is a sign with a wheat stalk on the door).

Only a few people could understand the first example: people who have lived in that particular village for a very long time. The second example, if translated accurately, is universal. Good technical documentation, translated well, will win every time.

Good Documentation in Action

Intuit, the popular tax-preparation software company, was able to reduce inbound support calls by 60 percent by offering simple things such as a frequently asked questions (FAQ) section on its Web site along with a knowledge tree (Sento Corporation 2003).The Intuit case is presented as a case study on the ContactCenterworld.com Web site. It is surprising how shocked the Intuit people were when a vendor was able to reduce their call volume through good documentation. The vendor, of course, had plenty of fancy names for its solution. True enough, a "blended approach" offering various forms of support while making it easy for the customer to resolve their own issues is the right way to go. The bottom line is Intuit just improved its documentation by making it more accessible. FAQs and knowledge trees are nothing more than fancy labels for technical documentation made available online.

Chat and E-mail

Some of you may be excited at this point, thinking that I have made a good argument for providing written customer support via Web center chat or e-mail. But this is recommended only if you can afford to have highly trained technical writers and a message routing system that ensures same-language interaction. Computer customer support is a good candidate for this approach. In most other cross-border scenarios, the additional context provided by the human voice will better facilitate the resolution of issues.

One note of caution: Groups of people who are in specific fields such as computer support often develop extreme skill levels in cryptic (high-context) message swapping in the form of abbreviations, acronyms, and smileys. Smileys is a whole topic unto itself. Creating smileys to convey nonverbal context in ASCII characters is an art form—a limited yet powerful tool to add context to an exchange. But because they usually represent facial expressions, smileys are a reflection of the culture of the person who creates it. Remember, smiles mean different things in different cultures. Asians sometimes smile to show unease, for example. A frequently used Japanese smiley looks like this: (^_^). The Japanese sign for "excuse me" looks like this: (^o^;>). The triangular shape on the right represents embarrassment—a way to save face for the other person (Pollack 1996). It is critical for agents to understand this and for policy to be set accordingly.

 ## TRAINING TIP

If your agents are providing customer service via text-based media such as e-mail or chat:

- Train them not to use smileys, abbreviations, or acronyms.
- Tell them to use short, simple sentences to make their points. One thought per sentence is a great rule.
- Make them aware of the permanent nature of text interaction. Have them assume that anything they type will be available for all to see.

In short, if your agents are providing text support across borders, train them to follow these simple rules, and they will be less likely to encounter difficulties with customers.

It is critical to test your agents' written skills thoroughly before allowing them to "go live" with your customers, because there is one thing about text messaging that is very different than your voice calls: It leaves a permanent visual record of the interaction. In call centers, we record conversations to track the quality of calls. But with text messaging, the balance of power is rapidly shifted to the customer. Every single customer has access to a very simple computer function called copy and paste. This function allows him or her to copy anything that flashes across the screen and share it with the whole world. In an earlier section, I discussed the prevalence of Web sites and bulletin boards that allow customers to complain about the service they receive. Guess what happens to the below-par customer service e-mails and chat sessions your agents send out? They get recorded for eternity in cyberspace. Therefore, you should think very carefully about the parameters of what agents are allowed to type into the instant messaging system and what the consequences to your company's reputation would be in a worst-case scenario. This is true for any text messaging service, including intraculture interaction. The danger with cross-cultural text communication is that you may not be able to imagine the worst-case scenario because it is difficult to know how something will be perceived on the other side.

Web Centers: Designing Customer-Centric Support Sites

While English is the lingua franca of the Internet, customers still prefer support in their own language. Therefore, most portal suites are designed to support multiple languages. They use database schemas to change menu language and content depending on where the customer is from. Do not take this capability for granted, however. Ask your vendor tough questions about how this works and how it is maintained. Good questions would be:

- How many languages does the system support?
- What version of a particular language is used—for example, American English, Castilian Spanish, Cantonese?
- Does the customer get the appropriate language automatically or through self-selection?
- How easy would it be to add new languages to the system?
- Are there expenses involved in adding new languages, or is that part of the normal upgrade cycle?

Taking care of the technology was the easy part. Now, you have to translate all your support documents in a way that is suitable for each language group. Remember that systems features, such as navigation menus, are not the same thing as support documentation for your product or service. Further, translating your support documents is not enough. They must be tested by real-world users in the same context that your customers will be using the information. The translator employed for the project should also be an expert in the subject matter. Still, take nothing for granted. Have it thoroughly tested and reviewed.

Beyond the text, ensure that the group who designs the interface in terms of color and graphics is representative of the end users. Colors carry deep symbolism in different cultures. Sometimes these meanings are subtle, but why would you not use colors that create a positive impression for your customers? Customer service portals often have pictures of attractive young ladies and gentlemen with headsets. Think very carefully about how you use these for your target audience. Sexy-looking women may not project the best image of your company if your customers are in the Middle East or North Africa. In Asian cultures, allowing your customer to interact with more senior, seasoned representatives of your company is a sign of respect. Age and seniority are very important in China, for example. If the models in the pictures are eighteen years of age, that may not be the best way to go.

The bottom line here is this: Do not assume that you know. Take the position of "I don't know, and I do not pretend to know everything." Speaking from experience, whenever I have been on Web projects that cross borders, I ensure that there is in-culture input and in-culture review before customers are allowed to use a Web portal. One successful strategy that I have used, especially in cases where a company does not have money to hire special consultants to test sites before release, is to make the new portal initially available to a limited customer segment. You could even alert that customer segment to the fact that the site is experimental and request feedback. If this seems unreasonable in your setting, offer some kind of rebate or upgrade as part of the trial.

The Intimacy Paradox

The telephone created a medium that was less intimate than person-to-person interaction. The telephone deprives us of visual cues, meaning there is less context available in the interaction. The Internet as we use it today is mostly represented in written language. Written language deprives us of even more context when compared to the telephone. The cross-cultural term for this phenomenon is *extension transference*—our tools remove us from the immediacy of the event, and we become like our machines.

It may seem as a paradox, then, that digital technology will eventually reverse this trend, creating opportunities for more intimate interaction across distance and time zones. One does not have to be a certified futurist with a Ph.D. to predict that, some day, customers and agents will be looking at each other eye-to-eye during a call through a computerized medium with a camera. It is possible already today, though not widely applied. The cultural implications of this will be very interesting. From what we have learned about the importance of nonverbal communication, this visual contact will dramatically increase the need for training as all those non-verbal cues will stream across the fiber and be interpreted, for better or for worse, by the customer and the agent alike. Accent neutralization does not change the color of a person's skin. How will customers react to that? If the reaction is negative, would we entertain using computerized avatars to ensure the privacy of the agent and put a more mainstream face on the company? Further, what are the ethical implications of going to those lengths to cater to customers in this manner? Even with the use of avatars and accent neutralization, we will now have to teach agents to greet Asian customers with a proper bow. What was once "put a smile in your voice" will become "put a smile on your face."

Perhaps some day we might even meet our customers on a virtual holodeck Star Trek–style. We may greet the customer with a full handshake. Where is that customer from? Better check the customer database. What is the proper greeting? Perhaps it is a bear hug or a kiss on each cheek, or is it three kisses? Whatever the eventual scenario, you can see that there may be countless opportunities for making the interaction more intimate and customer friendly, creating the ultimate customer service experience.

Part II

Culture, Communication, and Call Center Management

There is absolutely no inevitability as long as there is a willingness to contemplate what is happening.

Marshall McLuhan

4

The Power of Awareness

In Part I, we discussed the proliferation of call centers and how lowering the cost of providing customer service is critical in this competitive age. We learned that conflict situations happen because our beliefs, which are culturally determined, are different from one another's. In other words, because we are different from each other, we react to situations differently, creating conflict situations. Through illustrations and exercises, we saw that understanding one another's cultural differences is an important component of communicating effectively. And we took a look at the media and tools that we use to provide customer service, so that we might understand their limitations. Hopefully, we have gained some insight into the dynamics of the global call center business.

In Part II, we go inside the call center to explore some ways to improve customer service in cross-cultural settings. This chapter starts with breaking down the conflict situation and looking at it very closely, so that we gain an intimate understanding of how it works and how we can use awareness to diffuse it. Chapters 5 and 6 then focus on management strategies and training programs to reinforce our understanding of conflict avoidance and resolution in the call center environment.

Dissecting Conflict Situations

Understanding the psychological dynamics of conflict is the most powerful way to reduce tension in the call center setting. It is simple, and it can be taught to any agent anywhere. In fact, it is so fundamental that if you are learning this for the first time, you may wonder why you never encountered it earlier. The basic premise goes like this: Humans and animals have an innate need to communicate—not just to speak, but to have what we have just said be understood and responded to.

From a psychological perspective, communication confirms that we exist and that we matter. Nothing feels as good as the affirming smile from your mother, a friend listening fully to your problems, your teacher giving you an "A" on your test, the encouragement of your coach, or the returned affection from your loved one. And you can no doubt recognize the physical and emotional reaction you have even when just imagining these situations.

Now, consider not having those things. Consider instead zero feedback: not getting a reply from your mother, not having your friend return your calls, never having your test at school be graded, having your best efforts completely ignored by your coach, and not having your display of affection to your partner noticed or reciprocated. Even just reading about these scenarios, you probably have an emotional reaction. You may feel a strong tug in the stomach area. Or you may feel irritation, as you instantly dismiss the scenarios for fear of their overwhelming reality.

Now consider negative communication—sarcasm, angry words, uncontrolled sputtering, swearing. These are arguably better than no communication at all because they still involve *some* interaction. But I am sure you recognize there is a visceral reaction to negative communication just as there was to nonresponsiveness. Whether the feeling is a tug in the stomach, a sense of irritation, or even a "fight or flight" reaction, lack of the expected kind of feedback causes emotional discomfort of some kind. Certainly, the degree of discomfort will vary from situation to situation, from severe anxiety and depression to some mild nervousness or a dark thought that is difficult to fully describe.

Since these examples are of a personal nature, they may not appear relevant to call center operations. But, the chain of events that develops during miscommunication in the call center is exactly parallel. In the call center, we often just ignore the situation, and essentially learn to live with the problems, unless it escalates to negative communication. But that solution ignores the fact that even most subtle forms of pain create negative action and reaction, which are detrimental to both the customer's experience and the agent's work experience alike. That is why it is important that we magnify and explore even the slightest discomforts or negative reactions that occur in the call center.

Psychologists have conducted countless experiments documenting the cause and effect relationship between emotional pain and negative behavior. When I first learned about the nature of cross-cultural communication from Gary Weaver at American University, he used some eye-opening examples to illustrate this action and reaction:

- Two rats in a cage who are subjected to electrical shocks eventually attack and kill each other because they perceive the other has inflicted the shocks.
- A child who gets spanked by a parent kicks the cat afterwards as an outlet for shame and hurt.
- When the vending machine will offer neither a soft drink nor the money in return, our instinct is to kick it and push it with vigor (Weaver 1988).

In the call center, the chain of events is as follows:

Stage	Event
1	Communicating is a very basic human need—to be heard, to be understood, to be valued. This need is universal. We expect even subtle reactions as feedback in our daily communication.
2	When we do not receive the feedback we expect, we experience emotional discomfort. The discomfort may take the form of irritation, anxiety, stress, or frustration.
3	The discomfort, in turn, causes some form of angry reaction. This could be in the form of sarcasm, shortness, or condescension. Often this aggression is misplaced toward things that are unrelated to what caused it to begin with. We may not even realize why we are angry.

The subtle nuances that are part of even the briefest conversation can be understood in terms of this simple action-reaction model. In a call center that handles calls across borders, the person on the other end is likely from a different culture and sees the world through a different lens, making the prediction of any reaction complex. When conflict develops, your agents may not know which buttons have been pushed to cause the irritation.

There are a myriad of factors involved in every exchange. While it is helpful to know as many cultural traits as we can, the most important thing to understand is the process of how an angry reaction bubbles up to the surface. If you think back to that moment when anger sets in, it is instinctive. It is an animal-like behavior that has evolved over generations. Being aware of the potential for perceived miscommunication in the cross-cultural setting allows the agent to not react and offers an opportunity to diffuse the situation.

I want to take a moment to elaborate on this thing that we are referring to as emotional pain or emotional discomfort. This pain can be objectively experienced or subjectively experienced. It can manifest itself physically or emotionally. It can be real or it can be perceived as being real.

The pain that most often occurs in the interaction between a call center agent and a customer is subjective, and based upon the experience of the individual. It is emotional rather than physical and experienced through feelings. If the pain is particularly strong, it may result in physical manifestations, but this is the exception. Last, and most important, it is perceived. Let's contrast perceived pain with real pain. Both hurt, of course. The difference is that when you are dealing with people who are culturally similar to yourself, you are better able to distinguish between what is real and what is perceived. When you are aware of the difference, you are less likely to react negatively. To further explain the types of pain, refer to the following Summary of Pain Types table:

SUMMARY OF PAIN TYPES

Pain type	What causes it	How we react to it
Objective physical	Accidents, disease, and natural disasters	We may fear it, and it may cause us distress, but we are less likely to act out aggressively as a result of it.
Subjective physical	Inflicted by someone on purpose	Because we attribute the pain to someone, it is now twofold. You still have the physical pain, but you also have a subjective emotional pain. See "Subjective emotional (real)," below.
Objective emotional	Death in the family, normal work stress and anxiety	We know what causes the pain and we attribute no fault to what caused it. That does not mean it is not painful or that it will not cause a reaction. It is just less likely to result in an immediate acting out.
Subjective emotional (real)	Someone ignores you, someone treats you rudely	We attribute the cause of our emotional pain to something or someone, and we judge it as wrong. Then we attack it directly or in a misplaced way.
Subjective emotional (perceived)	Same as above, but it is not intentional. You think someone is mistreatingyou, but that party hasno intent to do so.	Although not inflicted intentionally, the pain you feel is still real and you react to it.

In any cross-cultural situation, it is important to constantly question yourself about whether your reaction is to real or to perceived events. Did the person intend to push my buttons, or is it merely my perception? A good example of this is empathy. When I tell you a story about my broken computer or my lost plane ticket, I am expecting you, the call center agent, to listen to me. Empathetic listening skills are imperative in providing good customer service. This involves acknowledging to the customer that you are listening to what she is saying. Unfortunately, the nuances of nonverbal empathy on the telephone vary greatly from culture to culture (it is high-context in nature). In Sweden, for example, empathetic listening involves saying yes *(ja)* with an inhale—a very strange sound indeed for the outsider. Americans are more likely to make *hmmm* sounds during a conversation to show that they are engaged. Replicating these displays of empathy across cultures is virtually impossible. So if I do not get the signals to which I have grown accustomed, how do I react? I will probably feel frustrated, as if you are not hearing what I am saying. Do you, the foreign call center agent, intend to make me feel frustrated? Absolutely not. You just don't know the subtle ways of showing me that you are listening. As a way around this problem it is recommended that agents provide a low-context verbal affirmation to the customer that expresses interest, understanding, and encouragement. Simply saying "yes, I understand" occasionally will be appropriate for most cultures.

Communication Breakdown: Some Examples

In applying these models to a few call center scenarios, let us first examine a basic interaction to see if we can break it down. To isolate the psychological component, we first examine a situation that has no cross-cultural complexity.

> *Joe and Jane are both Americans. Joe has a problem with his computer and calls customer support. Joe is not a highly technical person, so when he talks to the agent he describes what he is experiencing the best way he can. He describes what he did before the problem occurred, the blue*

screen of death, and so on. Joe is doing the best that he can to paint a clear picture.

The agent, Jane, cannot diagnose the problem. Before you look at the table below, ask yourself who gets irritated first and why. Whose fault is it that they are not communicating? Note that the descriptions of the scenarios are their descriptions of how they perceive and interpret the situation.

First, from Joe's perspective:

The breakdown	Emotional pain	Negative response
"I am really trying to tell the agent what is wrong. Why doesn't she understand?"	Joe feels general frustration and perhaps some stress from a sense of wasting time.	Joe feels a sense of shortness and irritability.

Now, from Jane's perspective:

The breakdown	Emotional pain	Negative response
"I am following the script. I just can't diagnose this problem. Boy, this person is rude!"	Frankly, Joe's rudeness hurts Jane's feelings.	Jane is now aloof and distant as a defense mechanism against Joe's rudeness.

Even a very simple example like this highlights important perceptual nuances. Joe has every intention of making himself clear, so we really cannot blame him for the fact that things are going wrong. The agent has failed to understand what Joe is saying. A more experienced agent would probably have had more success, because the more experienced agent has additional context and knowledge to interpret the limited information Joe provides.

Joe gets upset first because he is frustrated that Jane does not understand him. When Joe treats Jane rudely, he hurts Jane's feelings. That is Jane's pain, to which she eventually reacts. If someone treats you rudely, do you feel heard and understood? No. But the most important thing we must get out of this example is that it is the emotional context that will cause the reaction. It is all about the attributions we make to what is causing the pain, how we label it, and then how we react.

Recall the Afghan man and the German woman at the train station (from Chapter 3). This example highlighted some very applicable customer service elements. Now that we understand the action-reaction component, let's break down and analyze what happened in this instance. Again, the comments below are their reactions, not the things they say to each other.

First, from the perspective of the German customer service representative:

The breakdown	Emotional pain	Negative response
"I am telling this man how to catch his next train as clearly as I can. Why does he not hear what I am saying?"	She feels stress and frustration.	She uses an angry voice and behaves in a hurried and irritated manner.

Now, from the perspective of the Afghan traveler:

The breakdown	Emotional pain	Negative response
"Boy, I just cannot establish any rapport with this woman. She barely looks at me. She speaks so fast that I can't even understand her words."	He feels loss of face and some embarrassment because of the inability to understand the directions.	He makes a sarcastic remark about the long line being her problem.

The beauty of this example is that it shows how the action-reaction events work on multiple levels. This multiplicity is especially true in cross-cultural situations when we do not understand the context through which the other party perceives what is going on. When the German woman felt that she was not heard, her instinct kicked in. Without even knowing it, her pyramid of beliefs judged the situation and said "That idiot! Why does he not understand? I could not make myself any clearer!" That was her emotional pain shining through. His causing her pain is only perceived, of course. He has no intention to harm her in any way. The rest of the communication is difficult to predict. Everyone will react differently. She used an irritated voice, whereas someone else might shut down the conversation entirely. Then the Afghan man resorted to another form of aggressive behavior, sarcasm. His communication breakdown came in the form of not allowing them to have a complete exchange, dressed up with all the courtesies that he thinks are typically required.

Note that the mechanics of the previous examples are the same. Both people feel as if they are not being heard and understood. This is frustrating, and they both blame the other party. The concluding section of this chapter provides an illustration of the combination of cultural and topical context that the agent needs to be truly effective.

In the worst-case scenarios, miscommunication will result in the customer lashing out at the agent. As with the rats shocked in the laboratory, angry reactions are often directed at innocent victims. The rats did not know that there were scientists in white coats observing them as they were shocked with electricity. So they turned on each other. In the same way, the customer did not see that the agent was not the true cause of his anger. Screaming at a call center agent is a misplaced reaction—downright irrational in most scenarios. The call center agent did not manufacture the product. Agents often do not even really work directly for the company that made the product. But it is true that the call center is often the official face and sounding board from the perspective of the customer and, as such, it gets the blame.

Now, let's use a very simple example to illustrate how an agent who has been trained in cross-cultural communication skills might handle a difficult situation like this:

> *Meet Machiel. Machiel is a nice young man from Holland, where he works at the Widget Company call center. Machiel has been brought up to be kind and to treat people nicely. Machiel is not very comfortable with confrontation. When faced with confrontation, Machiel would rather choose flight than fight.*
>
> *Meet Bella. Bella is an Italian-American living in New York. Bella has been brought up to be a survivor in the hustle and bustle of New York City. She can fend off anyone, and a good time for Bella is a healthy shouting match with her friends at their local watering hole.*
>
> *Machiel and Bella are about to speak on the telephone. Bella has just come home from a long day at the office, and she is furious because a replacement widget she ordered from the Widget Company where Machiel works has not arrived in the mail. Machiel is working the late shift and things have been quiet so far. Bella picks up the telephone, ready to give a New York tongue-lashing to anyone who picks up on the other side.*
>
> *Bella is in fine form as she fires off her first salvo, about five sarcastic sentences lasting twenty seconds. As Machiel hears this, blood rushes to his head as the adrenaline kicks in. He wishes he had never taken this job and wants to immediately rip his headset off and go home.*
>
> *Luckily, Machiel is well trained. He allows Bella to finish and asks if he may put her on hold in order to check on her account. Before checking on Bella's account, he pauses briefly, just for a few seconds. He closes his eyes and, as he has been trained to do, observes his own emotions. He clearly sees his fear of engaging Bella. In his head, he says to himself, "Bella is angry, but it is my mind that has labeled her behavior and judged it as frightening. Therefore, the reaction to her behavior is my problem." Instantly, his awareness of his reaction diffuses his judgment of Bella. He proceeds to calmly handle the issue.*

Bella experienced the broken widget as a miscommunication because her interpretation is that the product does not work the way she was led to believe it would. And to make matters worse, she feels that the manufacturer is not standing behind its product by sending the replacement that was promised. This created irritation, and resulted in yelling at the agent. Then the agent diffused the situation by listening and taking corrective measures. This affirmative listening does not have to be a drawn-out therapy session. It is simply an acknowledgement that the agent heard what the customer said. That allows the two of them to move on to the next step.

Advanced Self-Awareness

As we have seen, there is an antidote for knee-jerk anger responses, which can easily be taught. That antidote is simply understanding why we react the way we do. One way to gain a deeper appreciation for why awareness is so powerful is to look at some of the teachings of Buddhism. These teachings carry a strong distinction between the manifested world of forms and the realm of being. Our minds are part of the manifested world, the physical world around us in our physical form. The essence of the mind is culture—the pyramid of beliefs that we learned in our youth. If you remember the definition of culture as communication, anything you do and say is a reflection of your mind and thus your culture: They are two sides of the same coin. One problem with beliefs is that we identify with them very strongly. We are under the illusion that our beliefs are who we are. It is an unspoken fear we all carry that if I could erase all your beliefs, I would annihilate you. Therefore we cling to our beliefs like precious gems. We compare them. Mine are better than yours. But are your beliefs really who you are? If you were adopted and raised by a family on the other side of the world, would you have the same beliefs that you have now? Would you still be you? You can see the conundrum. It is the old nature-versus-nurture argument that we have heard a hundred times before.

Viewing thoughts as impermanent objects, as Buddhists do, offers an interesting perspective for us in the context of this book. The number one priority in becoming an effective cross-cultural communicator is to be aware of our own belief systems. We have to learn to understand how our pyramid of beliefs dictates how we judge and react to the events around us. Buddhist meditation contains a simple strategy for observing your thoughts and recognizing them for what they are—thoughts and no more. There is nothing mysterious or very challenging about it. When a thought comes up, allow that thought to exist without judging it. It is neither good nor bad. Thoughts are impermanent. They come and they go. The key is to allow them to come and go without getting all worked up. Do not judge your thoughts. When we observe our own thoughts, this creates a tremendous opportunity to diffuse the chain reaction of communication breakdown, emotional pain, and aggression. In other words, by virtue of being willing to observe and be aware, we have created distance from the immediate reaction and an opportunity to respond from a fresh perspective—one that is not charged with judgment.

You can practice self-observation for cross-cultural application. Let's say you harbor a prejudice of some kind. Perhaps it is a behavior that annoys you or an ethnic group or a country that you are not particularly fond of. You know it is wrong to have such feelings, so whenever they surface, you reject them and dismiss them because, you say to yourself, "I would never think like that, not me." The next time a thought like that comes up, stay with it for a while. I do not mean cling onto it and identify with it. That is certainly not what I am advocating. Just understand that your thoughts are culturally determined. You were brought up to believe the things that you believe. Your beliefs may be right, and they may be wrong. By allowing them to *be* for a while, even the beliefs that do not align with your self-image, you might gain some insight into why they are there, which will actually diffuse them to some extent. Notice the charge behind the thought and the associated feelings they may generate. Notice how your beliefs are often associated with deeply rooted fears and desires.

When you have practiced self-observation a few times, you learn to catch yourself in the moment when you are making an on-the-fly judgment about a situation. If you are a customer service agent, you catch yourself as the conversation gets a bit emotional. Pause, observe, and understand that the reaction and the thought happened inside of you. You created it, but it is just a thought. As it came, it will go. By the very fact that you have a firm grasp of the cause and effect, you can take time out and think of better approaches. You just learned about this in the previous section. You learned the cause and effect between miscommunication, pain, and anger. Now, you just have to be aware on an ongoing basis. If somebody is pushing your buttons, it is probably because he or she has had his or her own buttons pushed. That is the way it works. People are like robots this way. We all have buttons you can push, creating all kinds of interesting reactions. It also helps to remember that as humans we fear being misunderstood—we desire to be understood. It is the fear and the desire pendulum that makes us jump to conclusions through assumptions or judgments rather than objectively focusing on what we know.

Putting Awareness to Work

"You have to be *fully* present," said an experienced call center manager as he motivated his agents. This guy beamed with positive energy so he could get away with this direct approach. His theory was that a customer can always hear right away if you are not really paying attention. Further, he said that forced alertness comes off even worse, because the customer can hear fear and negativity in the agent's voice.

You probably have agents who are aware and present like this naturally. Agents have told me that they have a second persona that they switch to when they are taking calls. This persona does not react to events the same way that their off-duty persona would. Reactions are more controlled because they do not take things personally. If a customer is upset, they focus on the practical matters at hand. They do not allow their "real" person to attach labels to the customer and descend into anger, blame, stalling, or other passive-aggressive behavior. This kind of coping strategy frees the agent from fear during the interaction. This second persona cannot be annihilated by the caller. It is detached from the rigid beliefs of the "real" person.

Ask yourself, do you not have agents like that? Are they not your best agents? Have you not had new hires who do not even make it through your induction training because they cannot go into customer service mode at all? This is all about training people to be like those best agents mentioned above. Also, your best agents will get even better because they will be more aware of what they are doing: going into that mode will become even more effortless, and they will become even more consistent over time.

Below is an illustration of the mix of resources that an agent has available to him or her during a call. They are a mix of learned skills and abilities and systems resources that need to be tapped into at various points. The purpose of the illustration is to help create awareness of the resources so that they can be used with maximum impact. It assumes, of course, that the agent has been trained in cultural awareness. Knowledge empowers your people to understand how different cultures interpret the world they see. Knowledge allows agents to distinguish between what is real and what is perceived. When you teach your agents and coach them on these topics, you equip them with the tools they need.

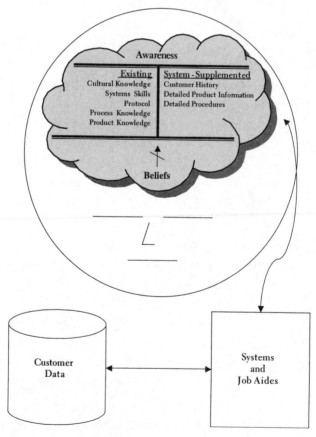

Agent Mind and Systems Resources.

1. On the top is awareness. This is the critical part of the illustration. The agent is aware of all the resources below, including the beliefs at the bottom.
2. On the left side are things the agent needs to perform his job. They need to be preexisting, for the most part. They are knowledge, skills, and abilities.
3. On the right side are areas in which the agent will need systems assistance to perform his job. Note that systems skills have to be there in order to tap into that information.
4. Beliefs, opinions, and attitudes are suspended, as illustrated by the arrow with the horizontal diagonal line.
5. The agent taps into all these resources, as needed, during a call.
6. Scenario
   a. Agent encounters a conflict situation in dealing with a customer.
   b. Agent immediately recognizes it, using his awareness.
   c. Agent taps into his awareness of his own cultural bias and diffuses his own reaction to the situation.
   d. Agent taps into additional customer history and his own knowledge of the customer's cultural background to come up with a strategy for handling the situation.
   e. Agent proceed to handle the issue using protocol, procedures, and systems resources.

If you are a call center manager, at this point you may say: "I can't train my agents on awareness, culture, beliefs, and all this other stuff. They will either dismiss it or they will not understand it." I can understand your reaction, but stop a minute and ask yourself if your response might not be the result of a few of your own biases. I grant you that this material may not be appropriate in all settings, but my experience is that all these concepts are easy to understand for most agents. The following affirmation exercise illustrates a way to accomplish some degree of the awareness and alertness that we are trying to achieve. I encourage you to modify the information in this chapter so that it fits well with the culture in your center. Use language that your employees will understand. Also, don't force anyone to accept the contents of this chapter as gospel truth. That would go exactly against what you are trying to get across.

TRAINING ACTIVITY: Affirmation

If a full training session on cross-cultural awareness is too much in your call center, try an affirmation exercise similar to the one below. Have your agents read this affirmation quietly to themselves prior to the beginning of every work session. Have them post a copy of it on their cubicle wall so that it is always available.

- Every person I will talk to has a different perspective than I do.
- I will not label and judge their perspective as good or bad.
- I will be alert, calm, and refrain from reacting emotionally.
- If I have an emotional reaction, I should kindly put the customer on hold and remember for a moment that I do not have to take it personally.

If your agents just giggle and dismiss this as psychological nonsense, explain to them that this is no different than the way athletes prepare by imagining themselves performing to their greatest potential. It is no different than the way sales people are trained to imagine the positive reception they will get before a sales call. It is no different than the way a priest meditates on the message before the sermon. This is simply a way to get ready for a live event and to project how it will all go successfully.

5

Creating a Customer Service Culture

It was about 11:00 a.m. and we had just finished a meeting in the conference room. The meeting was a postmortem about a training conference I had attended with two other colleagues. We were excited because we had just made contact with a lot of leads, and we were eager to begin the follow-up process right away. Just then, there was a knock on our front door. I opened the door, and it was a delivery agent from FedEx who was returning the crate containing our conference booth. The agent was perhaps twenty-five years of age and slight in stature, but she handled the 110-pound crate on a handtruck as if she was delivering a letter.

She smiled and said, "Where do you want me to put it?" "Right there," I quickly replied, pointing at an open area just inside the door. "I will take it from there," I continued in a grumpy sort of way, as moving crates around the office might possibly ruin my good mood. I had already spent plenty of time with that darn crate—packing it full of trinkets and dragging it around the conference area—to know that it was a heavy pain in the neck.

"No," she insisted. "I have it up on the hand truck now, so why don't you just tell me where you want me to put it?" At this point I was taken aback. She was absolutely correct. That ugly crate needed to be put away in our storage room, and I wasn't eager to do it. I obliged and led her to the back room. On the way, she explained to me that the lid was broken and that she had taped it up, but she recommended getting a new crate for our booth because tape would just not do the trick next time.

When she left, I was in a state of shock. What just happened there? I was in a good mood already, but she completely blew me away. It was just so rare to see someone who cared so deeply about doing a good job. I had not encountered that attitude in the longest time. I dismissed it as an anomaly and subconsciously categorized the friendly FedEx agent as "weird" until I read an article in a magazine a few days later.

The article in the January issue of *Business 2.0* was a short interview with FedEx founder, chairman, and CEO Fred Smith, entitled "How to Keep Your Company's Edge." Under the subhead "Make sure management is disciplined" was the following sentence:

> We make our managers treat our employees and contractors with dignity. They're not going to deliver the kind of service that FedEx is known for unless you deal with them on that basis.

In my head, I pictured the interaction between the FedEx employee and her boss on the morning the day our crate was returned. What might that morning have been like? What did they say to each other? Whatever it was, it set the tone for the employee's customer service that I experienced later in the day. As this chapter is primarily for managers on the floor of the call center, the lesson here is that we get out of our employees what we invest in them, and that this, in turn, is reflected in what the customer experiences. Because how we experience quality is subjective and culturally determined, this gets extra tricky when calls cross borders. The principal challenge for the call center manager is consistently the same, however: How do I treat, reward, and motivate my employees to optimize the customer experience? Simple as it sounds, this task can prove to be challenging.

The Power of Communication

I once had an instructor who taught that there is no direct correlation between employee happiness and employee productivity. He had studies to prove his point, and I believe it to be true to this day. Think about your own experience. There have probably been times when you have been very productive simply through encouragement and positive reinforcement. In that scenario, you were happy while you achieved great things. Then there were probably times when you were very productive only when under constant threat from a boss, a teacher, or a parent. In this scenario, you were probably miserable, but you still achieved great things. A recent exposé on a major American retailer with large manufacturing operations in China tells a grim tale of unsafe working conditions, long hours, little pay, and general misery. In one particular factory that makes cabinets for stereo equipment, a big banner on the wall read "If you don't work hard today, tomorrow you'll have to try hard to look for a job." Somehow, I have a feeling that banner was very effective in motivating the factory workers. I do not agree with it, of course, but I have a feeling it worked.

I introduce the above perspective here to show an appreciation for the fact that there is more than one way to get things done. The issues at hand here is how we define productivity in the call center and what management practices are best suited to improve productivity. Let's say you are the manager of a state-of-the-art call center. All the studies and measurements have been done. It is staffed with trained agents. Processes are in place. Still, morale is low, turnover is high, agents call in sick often or take stress leave. This in turn impacts service and the frustration level. What is going on and what can you do about it? How does a department's culture go bad? What was it that created an atmosphere where nobody cares, where people turn on each other? For answers we take the same psychological perspective as we did earlier, remembering that culture and communication are two sides of the same coin and that communication breakdown causes emotional pain and aggression. Here is the scenario:

A call center representative has not had a pay increase for two years. She has not talked to her boss for weeks. Several of her colleagues have quit. Obviously, nobody cares. She begins to "park" her line on an unused extension to appear busy.

What do you think would have happened if the agent's boss had stopped by her cubicle that morning and said

We have lost a lot of people lately, so I am really depending on you to help hold the line. I am trying to get a bonus approved for you because you deserve it. Keep up the good work. Oh, and I brought in some donuts. They're in the kitchen. Help yourself.

Do you think she would still have parked her line? It would certainly have been less likely. You as the manager create your department culture by what you communicate and how you communicate it. The way you make agents feel is how they will make the customers feel. What is more, when communication flows freely, your agents will be open to learn more about your operations and how to improve them.

Contrast these two action chains:

Culture	Communication	Agent Response	Quality
Positive	Communication is good. Agent feels valued.	Agent understands the importance of service level. There is a sense of ownership of the work.	Good service level. Good quality. Positive customer experience. Agent takes service level seriously and adheres to processes.
Negative	Little communication. Agent feels disconnected.	Agent does not understand service level and lacks a sense of ownership of the work.	Low service level. Quality suffers. Negative customer experience. Agent does not take service level seriously and may even cheat the system.

As you will see, the culture inside your call center has a direct impact on the how it performs. First let's agree that there is a universal truth regarding call center department culture no matter where your call center is located:

> Good customer service culture is one in which agents share the belief that meeting and exceeding customer expectations is important.

The employee who feels valued and connected to the company mission is a happy employee who is more likely to treat customers the way they deserve to be treated (regardless of the relationship to productivity).

This is a universal customer service principle. Now let's learn how this principle directly impacts the performance in the call center.

Quality and Service Level

As it turns out, productivity and quality are inextricably bound to each other in the call center, whether measured empirically or experientially. You can't have one without the other. There is no cheating or shortcuts.

In the inbound call center, we measure productivity in various ways, among them quality scores, service level, talk-time, and average time to answer. *Service level* (answering a certain percentage of calls within a certain period of time) and *quality scores* (derived from random customer response surveys) are probably the most common and most relevant metrics. We do not have space in this book to address all the technical aspects of call center metrics; suffice it to say that service level is an important metric that measures and reflects many aspects of call center operations. The formula is empirical, based on tangible measurements of time, but positive results are achieved through the efficiency with which an agent can create an appropriate experience for the customer.

In their book *Call Center Management on Fast Forward*, authors Brad Cleveland and Julia Mayben explain that you cannot have good quality scores without also focusing on service level and that you cannot achieve your service level without also focusing on quality (Cleveland 2001). This is true, because if you do not handle customers effectively by fixing their problems right the first time, they will call back, and your call volume will go up. If you do not answer the phone within a reasonable amount of time, your quality scores will suffer, since people just do not like being put on hold. This, by the way, is universal and it is a prerequisite for a positive customer experience. We cannot even begin to worry about customer *experience* until we get the basics of *service* right first. Whether you're from a Western, time-oriented culture or a more fluid, eastern one, no one likes waiting on hold for twenty minutes.

Quality is a different story in that how people perceive quality is culturally determined. It follows that the call center manager's role in running an international operation must not focus only on the mechanics of answering a call quickly. To achieve a high service level, the manager must also be concerned with the cultural motivations of the agents, the experiential triggers of the customers, and how those relate to each other. Cleveland and Mayben explain that in order to achieve a targeted service level it has to be

- realistic
- understood
- taken seriously
- adequately funded

This is a very powerful message, and I encourage you to read their book for a full treatment of how to achieve service level. In the context of call center management in a cross-cultural environment, I want to focus on exactly what you have control over and what that means for your management practices. In your current reality, you may not be able to impact what the target service level should be. That may have been determined by a different group of experts and executives a long time ago, and it may or may not be *realistic*. In addition, you probably have limited, if any, power to ensure that the target service level is *adequately funded* so that you have enough personnel and equipment to meet the demand. Sure, you can report deficiencies and write complaints to upper management, but you likely have no real power to appropriate funds.

The other two variables that enable call centers to reach their target service levels are most certainly things that are within the control of the call center manager: being responsible for ensuring that agents *understand* service level and that they *take it seriously*. Consider for a moment the complexities of explaining to your agents how quality is an important aspect of service level in the context of your overseas customers' cultural values. Can you do that now? What are the qualitative buttons that your agents must hit in dealing with the customer? Now, can you explain that in sufficient detail to allow the agent to take it seriously in the context of service level metrics? This is not an easy task, I assure you, but in the next sections I offer some practical suggestions for how this can be achieved.

So far, I have given examples of culture by country as well as by geographic region or group. Again, culture refers to a shared belief system that is present in nearly every aspect of a given society. Since belief systems are learned, people are products of their culture. And, of course, we know that corporations too have shared beliefs, as do departments within corporations, even you and your group of agents in the call center.

As with countries, a department culture manifests itself in everything it does. Every job done is a reflection of the department culture. I remember one group of just five agents who experienced the loss of one colleague and a new supervisor all within a very short period of time. The new supervisor was more hands-off than the former one, and the agent who left was replaced by a particularly negative person. He huffed and he puffed. Every little task was overwhelming, and he shared his laments generously. The atmosphere on that entire team quickly changed for the worse. Team members began avoiding each other. There was resentment because the complainer did not pull his weight. Unfortunately, the new supervisor did not intervene. It was not long before there were customer complaints. Interestingly, the complaints were not just about the individual problem maker. Certainly, that happened as well, but there were reported incidents across the board. The incidents did not have anything to do with *time to answer* or *talk-time* or any other hard metric such as that. The nature of the complaints related to poor quality of service, rudeness, incomplete answers, and poor follow-up. It was serious enough that changes had to be made, and quickly.

In this example, the culture of the team changed. The old positive beliefs were shattered through personnel changes and neglect. Agents began adopting a different perspective, and the customers could hear it right away. Because communication is so closely linked with culture, a call center's culture is particularly exposed for all to see. There is simply no way to hide your agents' feelings about their jobs from your customer because, as was said earlier, most communication is nonverbal, even in the call center.

There is a clear correlation between employee satisfaction and customer service quality scores in the call center setting. If you are training someone to go to war, you teach him or her courage and teamwork, and you want the rest of the world to see that your soldiers are fierce and brave. If you are training someone to provide customer service, you train him or her to be courteous, articulate, and skilled at resolving issues. You do this because you want your company to be seen by the rest of the world as positive and competent. Your agents are a reflection of your entire company. You, as the manager or the supervisor, are responsible for creating that reflection on a day-to-day basis.

About Banners and Bells

To motivate agents, call center managers in the United States sometimes use tactics such as hanging large, clearly visible motivational banners on the walls. Balloons may decorate the desks of top performers. When important targets are reached, a bell might ring, and everyone will stand up and cheer. These are motivational strategies that managers can put in place to get good results. Employees are excited and motivated, and, in turn, American customers get to speak to perky agents, which is what Americans like. Everyone is happy.

Such dramatics will not translate well in most other cultures outside of the United States. The balloons and the bells are a means to an end. They motivate U.S. employees and make them feel connected to the company mission. Try doing that in Germany. A former colleague from Germany had a term for it: the "Wal-Mart mentality," referring, of course, to the greeters at Wal-Mart stores who happily hand your shopping cart and cheer you on as you set off on your shopping adventure. I don't think Germans, in this case, are exactly offended by that enthusiasm. Most seem to find it curious, and perhaps there is a sense of pity for the person who administers the joy.

So, if banners and bells will not do it, what will? There is no quick and easy answer. As the call center manager, your goal should be to create a shared belief that meeting and exceeding customer expectations is important, but first you have to figure out what motivates your agents and factor in how customers will react to them.

To summarize, as the call center manager, you create the shared beliefs of your agents. We are talking about shared beliefs (culture) in the work setting. You are not changing who they are. The climate you create should correspond favorably to cultural characteristics of your targeted customer group. Communication theory uses the terms *encoding* and *decoding*. You want your agents to encode (create) their messages based on a set of beliefs that is familiar to the decoding system of the customer. To shape the beliefs of your team to suit the decoding system of your customers, you must learn to adapt your management style.

TRAINING ACTIVITY: What if You were Transferred?

Let us say your German colleague gets transferred to a director position at your call center in Indiana, where banners and balloons have worked well for many years. Upon arrival, she determines banners and balloons are expensive, all that cheering is distracting for agents handling calls, and she would rather rely on the agents' individual sense of responsibility for motivation. What would your reaction be? You are now confronted with a manager who is not adapting. She does not understand how things get done in Indiana. Yet, there she is—making decisions.

Likewise, if you get the director job in Hamburg, and upon arrival determine that this place looks awfully dreary and mandate banners and bells, your decision is not going to be received very well. When you are sent abroad to set up call center operations, whether it be Hamburg or Bangalore, you have to do your homework.

Adaptive Management Strategies

In the world of call centers, your people are clearly your main variable in creating success. Enabling groups of people to be successful is an age-old art of management, as evidenced by this simple but potent definition of management:

Getting things done through people.

That being said, management theory is notorious for being difficult to transfer from one culture to another. But that one little phrase holds true no matter what culture, no matter what language. Your job is to ensure that roles, responsibilities, and procedures are understood and that people are motivated to carry out their tasks.

From what you have learned about the relationship between culture and communication, there is no way to separate your communication with the agent from the agent's communication with the customer. How you get things done—your approach in managing your agents—will affect quality.

Much of the innovation in management theory has come from American schools. When foreign companies have looked for innovation in this area they have turned to the likes of Harvard and Wharton business schools and others to find models that will work in their settings. The results have often been disappointing, however. For example, matrix management has not worked well in a hierarchal society such as France. "Thinking out of the box" does not go over well in Japan, where the cultural norm is that "the nail that stands out gets hammered down."

On the other hand, situational leadership has been popular in management training for many years. It was pioneered by Ken Blanchard in his book *Situational Leadership*. The basic concept of this school of thought is that you, as a manager, adapt your approach to your situations. For example, if you have a group of employees that is not very motivated, you take a directive approach, giving clear directions. If your group is highly skilled and highly motivated, you let them go on their own.

TRAINING ACTIVITY: The Two Universal Management Concepts

The two universal concepts of management are

- getting things done through people, and
- situational adaptation.

Get a group of managers together and challenge them to discredit this claim. Ask them questions such as

- Are there any dimensions or aspects of management that do not involve communicating with and working with people?
- Can you think of any international management scenario in which it is not a good idea to adapt?

The ancient Chinese war strategist Sun Tsu said, "Know thine enemy as thyself." What do you think he meant by that? What if we say: "Know thine customers like thyself" or "Know thine agents like thyself." How do those sentences relate to the two universal rules of management?

While the ability to adapt to situations is an important skill on the management level, it is probably even more important for higher-level decision makers to understand what the management style of their managers is and how that style might go over in the setting that they are assigned to. Please note that I am really talking about situational *management* here as opposed to leadership. Leadership is a cross-cultural sticking point, because the traits we ascribe to our leader are culturally determined. I maintain that Mussolini would likely not have risen to power in Sweden.

To summarize my point, therefore, adaptive management is one framework that is universal in international business. Nobody can walk into a setting that is completely unfamiliar and expect to get things done just as he or she did back home. You have to adapt. Here is how:

If you are from	such as	dealing with a
Masculine Culture	Great Britain, United States	Feminine culture
Feminine Culture	Scandinavian countries, the Netherlands	Masculine Culture
High Power Distance Culture	France, Mexico	Low Power Distance Culture
Low Power Distance Culture	Scandinavian countries, United States	High Power Distance Culture
Face Culture	Japan, China, Spain	Non-face Culture
Non-face Culture	Germany, Norway, United States	Face Culture
Individualistic Culture	Australia, Germany, United States	Group-Oriented Culture
Group-Oriented Culture	China, India, Italy, Japan, Mexico	Individualistic Culture

The matrix below offers a helpful framework that you can use as a starting point to adjust your management approach. If you deal a lot with a particular cultural group, it is wise to conduct further research on that culture, beyond what is covered in this book. This chart introduces you to some areas to pay special attention to. Additionally, you can pick up important clues in the country assessments in Part III.

such as	you should
Scandinavian countries, the Netherlands	Respect the importance of consensus in the decision-making process. Avoid rushing and pushing.
United States, Great Britain	Engage rationally if faced with confrontation. Do not balk.
Scandinavian countries, United States	Expect rank to be broken. Think twice about making decisions independently.
France, Mexico	Be realistic about your position. Do not balk at giving clear directions to subordinates.
Germany, United States, Sweden	Understand the relative importance of face. If offended, do not react openly.
China, India, Italy, Japan, Mexico	Learn the nuances of face in that setting. Practice some restraint. Be aware of the importance of subtle non-verbal signals.
China, India, Italy, Japan, Mexico	Learn how to get accepted as a member. You are on the outside until you get in.
Australia, Germany, United States	Enjoy it since you can't escape it. Individualism is granted to you the moment you step off the plane.

TRAINING ACTIVITY: Adapting to Situations

Use the framework of the chart to work through your own situations. In addition, think of specific situations and see if you are able to come up with some answers for adapting the way you get things done.

If you are from _____

Such as _____

Dealing with a _____

Such as _____

In this situation _____

You should _____

This exercise can become the framework for discovering behavioral strategies for your agents in dealing with different customer segments in different situations. Once you have identified several common scenarios and agreed on good strategies, you can convert the table into a job aid that can also be used for training new hires.

Call Center Management—A Game Analogy

Once, I was asked to teach a course in call center management at a call center in Europe. The center was relatively new and was riddled with problems ranging from poor morale, frequent absenteeism, problematic relations between local management and management in the U.S.-based home office, and so on. Service levels clearly indicated that something was wrong. It was not unusual to see wait times of twenty minutes or more in some groups. Waves of U.S. executives had been visiting to try to rectify the situation to no avail. Behind closed doors there were talks of just shutting the operation down and routing all the calls to other centers.

Before my trip, I did my homework by debriefing various people on what was going on. What they told me was simply astounding. Groups of people would go on break together, leaving no one to answer the calls. Often nobody was monitoring the call queues, wait times, and service level. Of course, they knew better. The problems stemmed from poor morale and management's inability to coach employees to understand what their priorities were.

Stumped by the enormity of the challenge, I pondered how to get the point across that monitoring the call data and having agents available to respond was essential. Certainly, I was not going to be able to change their organizational culture in a few days. I had already been told what my reception would be like — "not another abrasive American coming over here to tell us what to do."

At last, it came to me. Soccer! Surely, this was one topic with which they could resonate. I created an analogy between call center management and coaching a soccer team. In the class, I asked who among them had kids. Several participants did. "Do they play sports?" I asked. Indeed, several did. "Do you attend the games?" Yes. "What is the coach doing during the game?" Silence followed for an awkward twenty seconds. "He is making adjustments in strategy," said one. I said, "Sure, but he is doing something more basic than that." "He is substituting players," said another. Again, I said, "Sure, but the coach is doing something more basic than that." Silence again. The silence lasted longer this time. Finally, I said; "He is watching the game! How can he make adjustments in strategy and substitute players if he is watching the clouds or taking a nap?"

I asked one of the parents who had children who played sports, "What would you do if your kids' coach was wandering around on the sideline and not paying any attention to the game?" His response was that he would get upset and tell the coach to wake up. Now it was easy to explain that the operations in their center were very similar to a game and that the play-by-play was in the call statistics from the automatic call distributor on their computers. Even more profound, in the game of call center management they were the coaches. I reemphasized the definition of their occupation as *getting things done through people* and the fundamentals of making tactical adjustments to personnel and priorities in response to call volume and call queues.

In a generally feminine culture, the people are not comfortable with the confrontational style of many American executives. Using tactics such as blame and threats created a disconnect that in turn caused the managers to withdraw and shut down to some extent. The feminine culture managers' behavior became clearly passive-aggressive. Their neglect was in effect a sabotage of company operations. Our training, along with other organizational adjustments, seemed to have a positive effect in the short term, though adjustments in corporate culture is something that takes a lot more effort than one training session.

The lesson to take from this scenario is that you really should find a way to frame your important messages in a way that your audience understands. This is an ongoing challenge, because you can't walk around telling soccer stories week in and week out. Adaptive management is not a onetime event. Adjusting on an ongoing basis also requires the awareness that we learned about in the previous section. You cannot adapt to something that you are not aware of. To be aware, you have to question all assumptions all the time. Of course, I don't mean every minute of every day. You would go crazy if you did that. Do it once or twice a day. In dealing with agent training or customer satisfaction issues, ask yourself questions such as

- What are my agents not hearing that they need to hear?
- What is it about my communication style that might hamper the message that I am trying to convey?
- What are we not doing that our customers want us to do?
- What subtle feedback did I get from colleagues and agents today, and do I know what they mean? Assume that you don't know, and then go and ask someone you trust if your interpretation of the feedback was correct.

Improving Culture (aka Communication)

Changing corporate or call center culture is the topic of many books. It is difficult to do and takes a long time. By nature, people resist change. Facilitating change often boils down to leadership, however. Somebody has to step up to the plate and create innovation in the organization's approach to getting things done through people. Remember, no matter what management level you are on, you can set the tone for how things get done in your call center.

How do you do that? Well, Sigmund Freud said that fear is the prime mover. Nothing will get people out of their chairs and pay attention like brute force. While you are not allowed to bring a weapon to work, you could yell and scream, threaten, ridicule, reprimand and make examples of poor performers, and take many other negative actions. However, what kind of culture are you creating if you are using negative reinforcement? You are creating a culture of fear and negativity, negativity that your customers will be exposed to and associate with your company as a whole.

In going about improving your call center culture, you basically have two approaches to choose from—directive or educational. The directive style implies giving clear directions without providing many of the reasons behind the directions. The educational approach involves teaching people about the nature of the problems that they face and suggesting possible solutions.

Because "good" customer service culture is culturally determined, the approach you choose (directive or educational) depends on where your call center is located and where your customers are. Generally speaking, the more masculine and the higher the power distance of a culture, the more comfortable agents will be with clear directions. The more feminine and the lower the power distance, the more comfortable employees will be with an educational approach. The education level of your employees can play a role here as well. More educated employees will usually respond better to an educational approach.

Remember that giving clear directions does not mean that you should be mean and militant. You can still maintain an open, positive flow of information and interaction while managing firmly and decisively. A manager can be benevolent and authoritative without being a disciplinarian.

Improving communication in the call center goes hand in hand with improving the culture. Agents who are happy and feel valued will provide higher-quality work. Your service level will improve. The following management communication strategies have proven successful in improving communication in the call center:

CALL CENTER MANAGEMENT COMMUNICATION

Start the day right	Start every day with a short meeting (breakfast, perhaps). Before the meeting, analyze yesterday's performance, so you can share successes and give recognition. Ask your agents what they think could have been done better. Give the group a short briefing on whether you are on target to meet your goals. Suggest some improvements. Teach them something about the call center every day.
Walk around	Be available, but do not be in the way. Be visible, but do not pry and spy. Be sure that the managers who do the walking around are ones who understand how the call center works. Managers from other departments and senior managers often misinterpret what they see on the floor. They think everyone should be on the phone. They do not understand the numbers on the board.
Encourage	Give a pat on the back. Write notes and hang them on their monitors. Write glowing e-mail. Post big banners. Give out chocolates. Give cash awards—anything that works in your cultural setting.
Acknowledge	Their main aspiration in life is probably not to be a call center agent, though it could be in areas where jobs are scarce. Find out what it is, acknowledge it, encourage it, and ask about it often. This shows that you are interested in them as real people. This approach may not work in all cultural settings. In France, for example, a clear distinction is made between one's personal and professional life. Asking about personal aspirations could be seen as prying.
Listen	Create ample opportunity to provide feedback. Encourage e-mail. Ask for verbal feedback. Make sure agents know their opinions are important. This may not work in high power-distance cultures (e.g., Mexico, France), where the employee expects clear directions from the boss with few questions asked.

Train	It is your job to ensure your people have the training they need to do their jobs. Track it. Require it. Set time aside for it when you schedule. There are cultural differences in how training gets done. (Please see Chapter 6 for more details about this topic.) Your insistence on the importance of training universally sends a message that you care about the work in the call center. That message in itself is sometimes a more important learning event than what happens in the classroom. Keep that in mind when deciding how much training you want your agents to have.
Advocate	Be on your agents' side by relaying their feedback to senior management. Senior management may not agree with all your requests, but your agents will appreciate your efforts and respect you for them. The alternative is that they see you as only a pawn of senior management—a prison guard looking for anything abnormal. This breeds distrust and will choke off communication. This situation is more true for low-context cultures in northern Europe and North America. However, hierarchal cultures still want their bosses to be benevolent in the sense that their boss is looking out for them.
Lead	Set high standards. Make sure that they are communicated clearly. Let the group know if the standards have been met. Be consistent and persistent about your standards.
Motivate	There are specific things that you can do to motivate and many good books on this topic. Get a book written for the local setting, however. Examples of motivational tools are contests, cash awards, prizes, and peer recognition.

Rewards Ratings by Culture

Rewarding desirable behavior is a powerful management tool. People respond to different things, however. Rewarding desirable behavior is a powerful management tool. It is my experience that people from different cultures respond to different things, however. It is in your best interest to hold focus groups and surveys to gain a clear understanding regarding how rewards are perceived in your setting. This is much more powerful than broad generalizations. For example, a culture may be very group oriented, but the immediate need is financial to support groups beyond the call center. In other words, the most important groups, from the individual agent's perspective, is not inside your office environment.

In every case, working rewards are positive communications that will improve your departmental culture, because communication *is* culture. As the department culture improves, you will find that you will need fewer such programs, because working in a department with a positive culture is motivating in itself. Group rewards will work better in some cultures. In fact, I have heard horror stories about Western-style individual rewards in places like Malaysia and Singapore. Let's say you are a vice president who is just passing through, and you have heard stories about one particular star performer in Kuala Lampur, and you want to give that person a nice plaque and a check. Not only could you rattle the person who is being rewarded, but the whole group will tend to freeze up. Remember, they won't want to cause you to lose face by disrupting the ceremony, so it may boil down to just an awkward moment that most people in the room want to get through as quickly as possible, including you.

Although individual awards are better in some cultures than others, a reward is a reward no matter where it occurs; it is better than no recognition at all. You can give anybody anywhere a check for $100 accompanied with a sincere thank you, and he or she will smile and come back to work more motivated the next day.

6

A Strategic Approach
to Call Center Training

For nearly all organizations, your people are going to be your most valuable asset. People are the competitive differentiator that will set your company apart. It follows that the things your employees know about how to innovate and deliver products and services are very important, and that learning must be a continuous priority.

Unfortunately, the call center industry appears to be averse to investing in agents and their training. In 2002, the Yankee Group conducted a survey that revealed 62 percent of call center managers believe training is their highest priority (Read 2002). In my experience, I have also found that the industry *believes* it is being strategic, but in reality it has a difficult time gaining a birds-eye view of how learning in the call center affects operational effectiveness. What this tells us is that managers on the floor know the importance of training. If they had the money, most would spend it wisely on empowering agents to help customers. They know that trained agents are happier and more successful, and they know that training works. However, from an executive perspective, there are tremendous pressures to lower costs related to customer service. So, while I am personally biased toward spending lavishly on training, the recommendations presented in this chapter take the executive perspective under due consideration.

This chapter is aimed partly at call center executives who allocate funds and partly at the call center manager who is responsible for ensuring that agents are ready to do their jobs. Both positions involve strategic oversight.

Granted, *strategic* is an overused word. It means having a purpose and plan and executing accordingly. Training, in particular, gets a great deal of attention as a strategic activity in organizations, largely because there is a consensus that there is little distinction between organizational learning and organizational development. It follows that we create customer service excellence in our organizations through customer service training. They are as closely linked as culture and communication, which we learned about in previous chapters.

As the importance of strategic learning programs are increasingly recognized, many organizations the world over are creating what are referred to as *corporate universities*. The term implies training with carefully considered outcomes in mind, usually closely linked to overall organizational goals. The term *university* is laden with traditional associations that are probably not very relevant to call center activities. I want to highlight this trend toward strategic learning, because I propose that global call center operations can benefit greatly from how top customer service organizations in other industries administer learning purposefully, methodically, and with long-term goals in mind.

For starters, training is known to reduce turnover. *Strategic* training programs have an even bigger impact on turnover. According to an article in June 2004 *Fortune Magazine*, companies that have implemented corporate universities have an average turnover rate of 13 percent as opposed to the 21 percent average (Field 2004). This is important, as the average cost of turnover is often calculated at time and a half of the lost employee's annual salary. Turnover rates in call centers vary greatly, depending on the use of part-time labor, which increases turnover rates, and on the intent and priority of each specific call center. In high-end call centers that emphasize customer service excellence, lowering the turnover rate is a critical ingredient to creating a consistent customer experience. From the employee's perspective, training is no longer seen as simply a benefit. It is rather a *prerequisite* that will allow them to evolve and get a better salary in the future.

Looking at a Role Model

The hospitality industry is an instructive place to look for a role model in the area of customer service learning. Perhaps the most recognized customer service learning program is the Disney Institute, one of the early movers in this arena. Anyone who is involved in the hospitality industry knows that having been steeped in the ways of Disney at the Disney Institute looks very attractive on a resume. Another stellar program is the Ritz-Carlton Hotel Company's Leadership Institute. Although the Leadership Institute's story has been told in articles and workshops repeatedly, I was fortunate to learn about it firsthand. It is an example of a strategic training program that the hospitality industry the world over holds as the gold standard in customer service excellence. Are you skeptical about using a hotel company as a benchmark for learning in call centers? Don't be. The Ritz-Carlton Hotel Company is the only company that has won the prestigious Malcolm Baldrige Quality Award for service—twice. To be sure, the Ritz-Carlton Hotel Company spends more on training than the average company. The average company spends 2.2 percent of payroll on training whereas Ritz-Carlton spends 12 percent of its payroll. What do they get for the extra money spent? While the hotel industry on an average suffers a turnover rate of 115 percent, the Ritz-Carlton rate is 24 percent.

What the Ritz-Carlton does that the call center industry can learn from is to create a customer service culture in a very deliberate way. In other words, they do not leave the creation of organizational culture to chance. They have an organized program at the corporate level, through which they place a very high priority on constantly implementing and reinforcing the values that create an excellent customer service experience. They have a credo, a motto, and an employee pledge that they consider as basic as their business plan. For new employees, they have an induction program with follow-up training and certification in each job role. Here they introduce their customer service philosophy, the Three Steps of Service. Further, they define their priorities in what is called the Gold Standard and teach employees about those priorities every morning in a short meeting known as the Lineup (Lampton 2003).

It is not the content of the Ritz-Carlton training program that we should learn from, though much of it is world-class. It is not the specifics of their particular organizational culture that we should look at as a role model, though that is certainly admirable as well. Rather, it is the ongoing passion for and priority placed on learning that can be replicated in the call center. Whereas other organizations write a credo and then never reinforce it, Ritz employees must carry it in their pockets all the time. While other companies say that learning is important, Ritz sets aside time every day, sending a huge message to its employees. Again, you will have to figure out exactly what kind of customer service culture you should have in your call center, based on customer culture and other priorities. The key point is to create an environment in which that culture is sustainable—and begins with commitment from the top.

Training: Cost or Opportunity Cost?

Now that we know what we want to achieve, how much should be spent to achieve the desired level of customer satisfaction? According to the American Society of Training and Development's *State of The Industry Report*, customer service agents receive the highest training expenditure of any employee population as expressed in percentage of payroll—a whopping 17 percent (Sugrue 2003). This statistic is interesting because it includes international data, but the number should be taken with a grain of salt. An agent who makes $20,000 per year would enjoy $3,400 in training benefits. Senior managers, who get an average of only 5 percent of payroll in training, would get $5,000 per year. Now, considering that the senior manager already has a master's degree, attends a conference or two per year, and may belong to a professional association of some kind to keep his or her skills up to date, the equation is more realistic. There is also an element of self-selection in the ASTD data since members provide the survey responses. Organizations that belong to ASTD, in my estimation, are more likely to care about training. This attitude could mean that the numbers reflect a more ideal picture than the reality.

A Yankee Group survey mentioned earlier in this chapter, reveals that half of call centers (including large call centers) put the annual training budget at $50,000. No, not per agent, but *overall*. The survey analyst concludes: "These low budget estimates indicate that even for large contact centers, training is not yet enough of a high priority to command a large budget, and more education is needed regarding the realistic costs involved with implementing training solutions" (Read 2002).

But is it really about money? Can money create a customer service culture in which the belief that "serving customers is important" is shared among all employees? So much of what the Ritz-Carlton does has nothing to do with money at all. We already established that Ritz-Carlton spends more than the industry average on training. But I will argue that many of the things they do can be replicated without adding a single cent to the training budget in your call center. It is simply a matter of changing the management philosophy toward one in which learning is emphasized, defined, and reinforced on an ongoing basis. It is a matter of fully recognizing learning as a strategic priority.

In the previous chapter on management strategies, I included a list of things you as the manager can do to improve morale in your organization. One of the suggestions was called "Start the Day Right." This is what the Ritz-Carlton does during morning lineup. Defining your culture and creating a forum for discussing what that means does not necessarily require a formal program like this. To be sure, it requires some time and space, and in that sense I concede that there is at least a moderate resource commitment involved. The cost of that time allotment will arguably be paid back through increased employee loyalty and commitment to customer satisfaction. However, this change in organizational culture can only begin to happen once we recognize that it is important. Then we can begin to define it and reinforce it. We can begin to learn about our beliefs so that they can be shared and, in turn, experienced by the customer. Regardless of what you have in your training budget, if you do not have that awareness and the intention of creating a great customer service culture, no amount of money will help you.

Creating a Framework for Call Center Learning

Every organization needs some kind of framework for learning. It does not have to be elaborate, but the organization should at least be able to complete the sentence "We train our people because . . ." This implies that there is a reason for training agents.

Ideally, the last half of the sentence should have something to do with the company at large. You might complete the sentence by saying "We train our agents because customer experience is our highest priority." Please ask yourself: What are we trying to do here? Using our previous example, if you ask an executive at the Ritz-Carlton Hotel Company, she or he will say they are preparing "ladies and gentlemen for serving ladies and gentlemen." If that does not impress you, the Kerzner Group, a properties management company that includes the exclusive Atlantis Resort in the Bahamas, aims to "blow the customer away." Both companies allude to what they are trying to accomplish with learning activities. Both acknowledge that the experience of the customer is somehow linked to the success of the company and that training is an important part of getting this done.

I would like to see the call center executive adopt this viewpoint. On a fundamental level, the priorities and the purpose of the call center executive should be deeply tied to the priorities of the agent who takes the calls. Both need to understand customer needs, products, and systems. More importantly, both must be open to learning about themselves, about customer needs, and about new products and systems.

Before we can build a strategic learning program, it needs to have purpose, and it needs to have some kind of shape. By shape, I mean a description of what the priorities are and who learns what, where, when, and why. Karen Barley, a recognized expert on organizational learning, often emphasizes the importance of building a learning structure that reflects the organizational culture that it serves (Allen 2002). This may sound unnecessarily complicated, but it does not have to be. For example, a steeply hierarchical organization might use a pyramid as a visual depiction of learning, with basic learning on the bottom, various layers of functional learning in the middle, and management and leadership represented in the tip of the cone. At the Ritz-Carlton Hotel Company, learning is represented in a flat, circular shape, as every employee has ownership and accountability for serving guest needs, no matter what their functional role. In this model, core learning is in the center of the circle, with various functional learning programs adding out and touching each other like layers in a cake (Allen 2002).

The model below is a visual representation of generic learning in the call center, with particular emphasis on the topics that have been covered in this book. This can be a starting point for depicting how learning happens in your setting. Please read about the components below and think about how they might be structured differently in you call center.

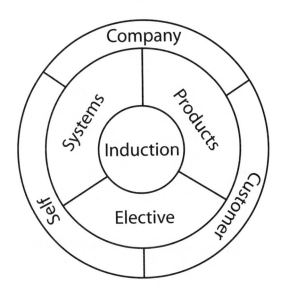

Call Center Learning Model

Core of the Model—The Starting Point
Core Learning
This is what the agent learns on the first day on the job. It includes basic information about the company and what it takes to be successful.

Middle Layer—What Employees Need to Learn Next

Systems Learning

This includes the trouble ticketing system, the customer relationship management system, and other systems that are utilized at your facility. Note that this layer also includes all the processes, job aids, rules, and so forth that the agent needs. Systems are not just computer systems. Call centers operate on an overall systems approach.

Product Learning

Learning about the product and service should be ongoing.

Elective

This represents something that you read in chapter 5. Most call center agents do not have their current job as their life ambition. If you recognize that and encourage some branching out into learning new tasks, it will do wonders for morale and retention.

Outer Layer—Cultural Awareness and Communication Skills

Please think of this layer as the communication and culture layer. This is the interaction with the customer. These are the all-important soft skills.

Self-awareness

Your self-awareness is learned through cross-cultural training.

Customer Culture

The agent learns awareness of the customers' culture and preferences.

Organizational Culture

The culture inside the call center, what it stands for, the image it projects, and how that relates to the employee and organization at large is made clear.

I encourage you to adapt this model to your setting. Make it more specific to your learning needs and the culture in your organization. If learning is important, it has to be marketed and promoted. Learning and reinforcing organizational culture and organizational change are intricately linked, so why would you want to leave something as important as that to chance? Give it a purpose, give it a shape, and communicate it clearly. These are the activities that will build shared beliefs—shared beliefs that serving customers is important work.

A Systems Approach to Learning

It is true that training is something that we do to get our agents to use the systems in the call center. However, we are not talking about reactive, occasional training, but about strategic, ongoing learning. For learning to be strategic and ongoing, we need a systems approach to sustain it. By *systems approach*, I mean that there has to be a method in place to assess needs, track progress, and measure outcomes. Anyone who is familiar with call center management should be very comfortable with this idea. We are going to treat learning in the call center as we treat our other activities. We are going to track it, evaluate it, and adjust it as time goes on. Below, I discuss some high-level aspects of strategic learning that call center executives and managers should be aware of, as they potentially have a great impact on how effective your operations are.

Evaluation

Any strategic learning program worth its salt considers evaluation before designing the program. Earlier, I asked the question "What are we trying to achieve here?" Now we must take that question to its logical next step: "What is it that I can measure in order to know that I am achieving what I am intending to?" This concept is nothing new. In fact, the Kirkpatrick Training Evaluation Model, which I favor among the various quality-and-return-on-investment models available, has been around a long time now. In my opinion, it is so robust that it will be around forever, and I feel it fits very neatly in the call center setting. I would venture to say that call centers are very sophisticated when it comes to evaluating how effective their operations are. The extent to which organizational performance can be attributed to training is a different question. The table on the next page explains Kirkpatrick's approach to training evaluation, how they can be measured in the call center, what metrics can be used, and some considerations about how to apply this approach in your global operations.

The bottom line is as that we are hoping to achieve some kind of business impact through our training activities. The Kirkpatrick approach allows us to track the ripple effect of training from the training event to our ultimate intended outcome. As a decision maker, you need to be aware of what the measurable variables are. Are they quality scores? Are they customer retention? Are they operational savings? Understand what it is you want to do; then decide how you want to evaluate it. This will allow you to hold your training department accountable for its activities.

It should be noted that many good call centers already perform level three and level four evaluations (described below). This is something that most other business segments only dream about. Level three and four refer to converting the obtained knowledge (from training) to behavioral changes

THE FOUR LEVELS OF CALL CENTER TRAINING EVALUATION

Kirkpatrick	What is measured	How it is measured
Level One	Learner reaction	Training evaluation (smile sheets)
Level Two	Learning/retention	Pretests and posttests
Level Three	Learner behavior	Quality monitoring
Level Four	Business impact	Customer surveys Customer retention Other hard business data

(Adapted with permission, Donald Kirkpatrick, 1998)

that have an impact on the company bottom line. As a call center executive, you may be surprised to find out that your business unit is much further ahead in this area than other business units.

Needs Assessment

The next tangible step in the systems approach to learning is to conduct a needs assessment. In short, we have to find out *who* needs to learn *what* in order to achieve our goals. Remember that the aim here is to create a complete learning program and a learning culture, not just a few courses scat-

Call Center Metrics	Global Variables
Same as any other training setting	Is this important in the local setting? Is it important for a learner to have a positive experience in the learning process?
Same as any other training setting	I would have to speculate that learning retention is universally important. Perceptions about testing may vary by cultural group, however. I would call testing a masculine cultural trait that is more common in the United States and the United Kingdom than in most other places.
Agent ratings based on quality scores	We must define the agent's behaviors based on what the customer perceives as positive.
Customer satisfaction scores	The key here is to define satisfaction as specifically as we can as it relates to the customer's culture.

tered here and there. Your learning is for your entire call center program and not just to provide a few reactive courses to solve this or that problem. There are several ways to go about conducting a needs assessment. Here are a few:

1. **Manager's advice.** Simply ask the managers and the team leaders in your center for their input on the training needs. They usually have a good idea on a practical level about what agents need to know to do their jobs.
2. **Define skill sets.** A more systematic approach would be to define the exact skills and abilities that are needed in each location and then test your agents against those skills. Testing will reveal the knowledge gaps that need to be addressed through training and coaching.
3. **Surveys.** You can survey customers about what they find to be important traits in customer service interactions and use these surveys as a basis for what agents should learn. Though it may be better to do this in an indirect way, you can probe for attitudes and perceptions regarding cultural groups. Surveys can also be conducted to sample knowledge and skill levels among managers and agents. Your quality surveys may indicate where there is a need for training. For example, if one call center is receiving markedly different scores from country to country, this may be an indication that agents need special skills in handling the customers from the country with low scores. You can also design a survey and distribute it among managers, support staff, and agents.
4. **Focus groups.** You can conduct focus groups with managers, agents and customers to arrive at the same results as discussed in number 3. Even brief and informal stories reveal anecdotal information that might otherwise be difficult to capture and that can be very valuable.
5. **Industry benchmarks.** Benchmarking and best practices are available through any number of call center and training trade associations. There are also consulting companies that specialize in facilitating benchmarking and gathering information about industry standards. If you are on a low budget, you can simply call colleagues you know and ask. You will be positively surprised at the level of cooperation that you will get. Remember that benchmarking is a two-way street. If you want something, be ready to give something in return. It will help you get what you need.

The fact that you are running a global call center operation makes the needs assessment process more challenging. The following Training Needs Assessment Table will help you analyze who needs what type of training in your operations. Think of the roles of agents and managers and how they impact operations and customer experience as you read the table.

TRAINING NEEDS ASSESSMENT TABLE

If	then the Manager	then the Agents
the call center is domestic, serving domestic customers	understands customer expectations and agent motivation	understands customer and management expectations
the call center is domestic (within your native cultural setting), serving foreign customers	understands agent motivation but needs training in customer expectations	Understands management expectations but need training in customer expectations
the call center is abroad, serving domestic customers (for example Indian center serving U.S. customers)	from United States— understands customer expectations but needs training in agent motivation from India—understands agent motivation but needs training in customer expectations	needs training in customer expectations and may need training in management expectations if out-of-culture

You can capture a summary of your analysis in a table like the Training Needs Report on the next page. Remember that support staff should not be overlooked. There are many instances where a culturally aware support staff is vital. For example, technical personnel have broad responsibility for setting up the infrastructure to support your call center. This often involves traveling to evaluate sites, meeting with vendors overseas, and resolving issues on a dispersed infrastructure with peers around the globe. In my experience, technical personnel have come up with some of the most relevant operational improvements as a result of cross-cultural training.

TRAINING NEEDS REPORT

Country of Operation	Management + Leadership	Agent Training	Support Staff
United States/ Atlanta	Coaching skills for team leaders Communication skills for senior leaders	Systems training A Product updates Dealing with colleagues in the Philippines	Systems training B ACD Configuration, Metrics and Analysis, Technical Writing
Philippines/ Manila	American Business English Product Training	Accent training Cross-cultural communication	Systems training A

Learning Management System

The Learning Management System, or LMS, does for learning what the Customer Relationship Management System does for managing your customers. Another analogy would be that LMS does for learning what your ticketing system does for managing customer issues. It is simply an augmentation to your existing human resources information technology infrastructure that helps ensure agents, managers, and executives learn what they need to learn to do their jobs. Currently, there are about one hundred viable LMS vendors out there. Suffice it to say that there a wide range of features and cost scenarios available in implementing an LMS solution.

My general recommendation is to shop around carefully and to be keenly aware of exactly what your needs are. In most call center settings it is important for the LMS to track e-learning so that you can ensure that refresher training or new product training that is often provided via e-learning is actually consumed by the agents who will talk to customers. As you are operating globally, it is also a good idea to consider a solution that uses a Web browser interface and that is not restrictive in terms of access from distant locations. Many vendors also act as Applications Service Providers (ASPs), meaning they can host the application for you, and make it accessible from all your call centers. The advantage of having an LMS is that you can measure training participation and knowledge acquisition through testing modules.

The LMS does many other things, including managing classrooms, instructors, materials, and e-mail notifications. To me, the systems approach and the LMS are closely related. The technology is no panacea for all your learning needs, but it is a tool that, when used correctly, allows you to operate strategically, especially when your operations are large, dispersed, and complex.

Training Modalities for Global Call Centers

Call centers are lucky because in some ways they have a captive audience. Therefore, there is less of a need to motivate agents to take training. In my experience, agents generally will take training as offered, scheduled, and dictated. That is not the case in every industry. Nevertheless, there is still a need to consider training modalities. By modalities I simply mean how learning gets done. This includes classroom training, e-learning, learning by doing, and coaching. Each has its strengths and weaknesses, but as we consider them, we must remember that, in the end, we are trying to create the most effective transfer of knowledge with the greatest amount of impact, at the lowest cost. In the call center environment we also have to weigh the importance of product and systems training versus soft skills training. We also have to remember that individual learning styles vary, so before we decide on a training program, we must first of all know our audience. In the global setting we have to add the fact that agent learning styles vary by culture. In large, dispersed companies, therefore, it makes sense to create training programs that are portable across many locations. Let's consider each set of variables.

Classroom Learning
Classroom training needs little explanation. We have all experienced it in our own lives and know that it is only as effective as the instructor. Generally speaking, most training experts agree that induction and soft skills train-

ing are best done in a classroom setting. Trainers are available from a number of companies, but these programs tend to be very costly and the experience offered by these sessions is very difficult to standardize, particularly if you are operating in a number of locations or over a number of shifts. One of the factors involved is that the amount of material that can be covered is very dependent on the skill level of the audience.

E-Learning

Many call centers are deploying e-learning as a way to lower overall training costs. Here, most training experts agree that product, process, and refresher training can be very effective using e-learning modules. It may not be the best choice for induction training, however. Consider this scenario, if you are not convinced:

> Let's say you need a paycheck and the best available job for you in town is at a call center. You know that they are hiring, so you go there to fill out an application. A week later you have an interview, and you are very excited to have a job. On your first day, you are welcomed by a representative from the human resources department. This person shows you to your new cubicle, gives you a log-in to your workstation, explains the basics about the headset and other equipment, and says, "Please take the first five modules of this training program. After each one you will be given a test. If you fail a test, you must take the module again and then take the test again until you pass all five tests. Please come and see me when you are done. Your team leader will then give a you a few pointers and you will be ready to take calls."
>
> You, being highly motivated, diligently take all the tests. You find the last one to be tricky and confusing, so you take it twice but are still a little stumped by it. However, your team leader explains that the topic that is confusing to you is confusing to everyone. If you are confronted with an issue related to it, you are to put the customer on hold and read the online job-aid to find the resolution. You get a pat on the back, a "good luck," and off you go.

How do you feel now? Do you feel like you belong? Have you joined the team? Do you feel any sense of ownership regarding this new company? Do you care about whether the company will do well or go out of business? Are you motivated? Are you making plans for the future based on all the opportunities that have been laid out before you? Do you brag about what you do for a living to your significant other? Are you passionate about helping customers? Are you looking forward to tomorrow? No? Wow, big surprise! E-learning is simply not the answer to every training need in the call center.

In my opinion, e-learning alone cannot provide a complete training solution. Learning involves give and take, feedback, correction, experimentation, and reward—communication, in short. Earlier in the book, we learned that people need to be heard and valued. We also learned that most communication is nonverbal. How much feedback does the e-learning system give you? You either passed or failed the test. That is the end of it, which is next to absolutely nothing in terms of feedback. Some systems exist that allow agents to record interactive scenarios with a computer voice. These are very useful but not very satisfying. Some even offer avatars that are almost lifelike, but would it not be a lot more exciting to reenact those scenarios in a group setting? Other programs entertain through very funny scenarios. Entertaining is good because we do not fall asleep, but it is not necessarily meaningful.

Learning by Doing
Learning by doing is a modality that can be a useful part of call center training. For example, once an agent has proved to possess adequate initial product knowledge, he or she might be assigned to first-level in-country support on that product. The one caveat that must be considered is that every interaction with a customer creates a lasting impression on both sides. Not only do you not want to create a bad experience for the customer, you don't want a bad interaction to taint the agent's view of his job. You must be cautious that your agent-in-training doesn't step on any land mines, and here the use of coaching may be an important training tool.

Coaching
A team leader might assign the agent-in-training on a particular product line to an agent, a coach, already experienced in that line. An opportunity might be provided to listen in on the interactions of the experienced agent with

time between calls for questions. Or perhaps an in-house program can be developed with the assistance of your most experienced agents that would provide role-playing scenarios for new or less experienced agents either one on one or in small groups. Careful attention, however, must be paid to the dynamic between the agent-in-training and the intended coach. Not all pairings are ideal, and management has to monitor progress with this in mind.

A Blended Approach

All these pros and cons make it hard to choose the best option. The answer offered by nearly every training expert on the planet is what is known as "blended learning." This term means that multiple learning modalities are blended into the total learning experience. For example, learners might take some e-learning in preparation for a live training event, allowing the basics to be covered more cheaply to allow for a more intense and effective live training session. In truth, nearly all training is blended and always has been. What is different now is the addition of e-learning. Go ahead, then. Blend it in and save some money in the process if you can, but don't believe it if a sales agent from one of the big e-learning companies tells you that you can replace all your training with e-learning. You could, but it wouldn't be wise. The real power of e-learning for global call centers lies in being able to roll out new information to agents all over the world simultaneously through the creation of one or two learning modules accessible on site, wherever that site may be.

Once the learning modalities issue is decided upon, the next set of variables is product and systems training versus soft skills training. As most agents need both, and because learning is continuous, make sure neither is a one-time event. I have seen environments where agents learn products and systems first, and then soft skills as an afterthought. In other companies I have seen soft skills covered first for agents who will do first-line responses in which very little problem solving is involved, with product knowledge added gradually as agents grow in their positions. There is no set answer as to which is preferable. It depends upon your product line, your employee culture, your customer culture, your facility, your selection of training modalities—in short, you have to look at the totality of your operation before you decide whether products and systems or soft skills should be covered first. And again, neither is a one-time event. Learning should be continuous and strategic, even in the call center.

Individual Learning Styles

In previous chapters and sections we touched on the importance of being aware of the culture of the customer and the traits of your own cultural group. Think of those as the macrolevel of cultural awareness. Then we discussed the culture in the call center, the organizational culture that we could label the intermediate level of culture. We have already discussed individual cultural awareness as being the starting point for being a good cross-cultural communicator. Now, let's focus on individual cultural traits as they relate to learning. Clearly, people have different learning styles. Some are more visual learners, others more auditory learners, and some prefer to learn by doing. Professional trainers are taught to observe these differences in learning styles and to adapt to a group accordingly. The skills required to do this are very similar to the skills of a manager who adapts his or her management style depending upon the individual or group. As an instructor, you also have to adapt according to cultural setting. Things such as group activities, rote repetition, self-directedness, presentations before a group, perceptions about the teacher, and more, vary greatly from one place to another. Here are some examples:

In feminine cultures, such as northern European cultures, learning is a very egalitarian group process. The expert is a peer. Participants' views are important and should be heard. Still, the individual has selfish motivations for participating in training, as it could lead to career advancement through new knowledge. The trainer in this setting should avoid appearing to preach from a podium. It is much more important to create a safe atmosphere where everyone is valued. That said, feminine cultures such as Sweden and the Netherlands are also very keen on facts and science, so the instructor must be prepared to support his claims with data.

For Westerners providing training in group-oriented cultures, it is often very difficult to adjust the teaching style. What do you do when you ask a question to the class as a whole, and nobody wants to answer? The answer is that if you want them to participate, you may need to create some activities that will allow the individual to communicate as a group member rather than as an individual. How do you react when your attempts to establish peer rapport are met with a loss of interest? The answer is that learners in group-oriented cultures tend to want to see the instructor as an expert. So if you want their respect, you may need to establish your position authority from the outset. As an example, I sonce lost rapport with a group of French students because they had written their names on their name plates last name first, first name last. I proceeded to call them by their last name as if it was their first name. From a French perspective, that is much worse than saying, "Hey! Granered!" would be in America. It was an embarrassing oversight for me, but I also lost their respect, and I maintain a lot of learning that could have taken place that day did not.

Learning priorities differ so much from culture to culture, it is hard to even begin an adequate discussion of them. Latin and Arab cultures often emphasize memorization or pure deductive reasoning. American schools often emphasize what is loosely called "problem solving." Problem solving, at its worst, is almost a Machiavellian learning style involving an inductive process where the ends justify the means. In other words, it is okay if we missed a few classical theories and techniques along the way if in the end we "build a better mouse trap." This would be viewed as sloppy at best by the French. I know an educated French woman who nearly pulled her daughter out of public school in the Washington, D.C., metropolitan area because of what she perceived as the sloppy, useless nature of "problem solving."

In any case, learning is a culturally determined process. Therefore, it is often is a good idea to have a native of the target culture facilitate the training. In running global operations, however, we must be ready to set the high-level priorities for the entire organization. For example, if I am responsible for customer service operations for a luxury good and my customers are very sophisticated, I must be able to say that every customer is an individual who will get the ultimate customer service experience. I also must have the wisdom to know that this means I may not know what the ultimate customer service experience is for all my customers. I, as the customer service executive, have to rely on a lot of good people in the field and in call centers to translate my priority into customer experience.

The goal of cross-cultural training is to get your people to be "consciously incompetent"—essentially the same as being aware—and to be comfortable with that (Craig 1996). The consciously incompetent person is the ideal learner; he or she is already fully aware she needs to learn. A very open exchange of questions and answers will work well with this type of learner. This learner is usually highly motivated, so you can give self-directed lessons to him or her as well. A big part of being aware is understanding and being comfortable with being consciously incompetent, essentially acknowledging how much you don't know!

 ## TRAINING ACTIVITY: Say Something Nice

Much of the training I have provided deals with the concept of creating a customer service culture, an environment in which the importance of serving customers is a shared belief. This requires a thorough appreciation for how culture operates on several different levels—individually, organizationally, and nationally. As a way to create an appreciation, I often start a class with an icebreaker exercise in which every participant is asked to say something nice. After introducing themselves, they can compliment my tie, thank a colleague for some help that they provided last week, thank their boss for giving them a break, express gratitude for the recent rains that have benefited their gardens, or anything else of a positive nature. After everyone in the room has said something nice, the atmosphere is positively electric. Most people are smiling. Some may be near tears for the wonderful words said about them. Without going into theory of any kind, I ask the class to remember the wonderful atmosphere that we created together, promising that later we will find out how it was created, so we can make our workplace a positive environment like that every day.

*   *   *

In conclusion I want to offer what I call the Three C's of call center train-ing for international operations. These are simply three key topics that I want you to keep in mind to ensure the training you offer is suitable for your organization. They are Continuous, Contextual, and Cost-conscious. *Continuous* refers to what we have just covered: learning is not a one-time event. *Contextual* refers to everything we have learned about culture, customer culture, call center culture, and how they relate to each other. The culture pieces should fit together and make sense as part of your strategic learning. Last, we cannot forget that call centers are cost centers. Therefore, our training activities must be *cost-conscious*. There are many ways to reduce cost of training: scientific staffing approaches, careful curriculum review, technology selection using realistic criteria, and an attitude that teaches coaching, management, and even doing the actual work as learning events. If you keep those Three C's in mind on an ongoing basis, you will increase your chances of success.

Part III

Designing a Global
Call Center Strategy

If you find yourself in the forest and you encounter a bear, that is not a problem. It is a situation that requires some kind of action.

Eckhard Tolle

7

Culture as a Competitive Variable

I n Parts I and II, we learned a bit about the global call center phenomenon, with special emphasis on the important impact cultural communication skills is on the customer and agent experience alike. We
also learned how to train and motivate agents in a way that allows for cultural variables. Now you may be asking yourself whether you should outsource all your operations to Bangalore. Probably not, but many would
think you would not be unreasonable to consider it. Some of the news coverage exaggerates the outsourcing stampede, however. We are made to feel
as if everyone is doing it, so we better get on board or be left behind. But
good managers never follow the lemming example; rather, they step back
and think carefully through their own situation.

Do the Right Thing

The goal should be to outsource the right call center operations to the right
location, ensuring that agents in each location are talking to the right customers at minimal cost. Just as every other industry has adapted to globalization, so will the call center industry. In the 1980s there was concern that
Japanese car companies would put Ford and GM out of business. As it turns
out, cars are still manufactured in Europe and North America, but now
they are also made in Japan, Korea, Mexico, Brazil, China, India, and elsewhere. Car parts literally come from all over the world. As in any other

industry, striking the right balance regarding *what gets done where by whom* is a constant challenge. Analyzing the current situation and trends has to be built into the ongoing business planning process. In the end, it is better to gain your competitive advantage from well-informed decision making rather than from quick fixes based on fads. *Doing the right thing* means not reacting and following everyone else. You should do what is right for your business. For example, who would have thought that it would be advantageous for Honda, Toyota, and Nissan to assemble their cars in Kentucky and Ohio? Well, it is, and they do. So too will this be the case in the call center industry. I have no doubt that many call centers in the United States and Europe will remain viable and competitive.

When it comes to deciding whether to offshore or outsource your call center operations and where your call center should be located, there are no standard answers. What follows here is not a complete treatment for making the decision either. But as a good reference for beginning your investigations, I want to recommend a white paper called "Improving Call Center Performance Through Optimized Site Selection" (Anton 2002). It introduces a comprehensive data-collection framework that I wholeheartedly agree with. The paper includes demographic information such as average age, salary, schooling, other industries in the area, and many other factors that should be collected and weighed against other locations.

As I have said previously, you could locate a call center nearly anywhere. Just because everyone else is heading to India or the Phillipines does not necessarily mean that it is the optimal location for you. The ideal location for your needs could be a completely new site where wages are low and skills are adequate for your needs. Good advice is certainly important, and there are many consultants who specialize in site selection. If you want to do your own legwork, among your best resources are local chambers of commerce. They can find local points of contact who will work with you to craft a solution. The purpose of Part III is to introduce culture as perhaps the most important variable in the decision-making process.

A Formula for Success

Many outsourcing ventures fail. One industry veteran, Juergen Reiners of Hewlett-Packard, puts the number at a 50-percent failure rate. In an interview in *Workforce Management*, January 2004, the interviewer presses him on that number. Could it really be 50 percent? Reiners insists and proceeds to outline the reasons. Most projects are sabotaged by executives before they begin. The business segments that are being outsourced are low on the priority list. Therefore, they do not get the proper time and resources to be successful. Managers who are not qualified get the assignment to manage what is a very complex venture (Meisler 2004).

For most companies we know that customer support is not a core business. The lure of low wages inflates the apparent opportunity for saving money. This, in turn, leads to bad decisions, and then the wrong people are assigned to the task. So what is a formula that works? The formula for success is basically the opposite of this scenario. It is so simple yet so hard to execute in the real world. Experienced people must be given time and resources to analyze the options in order to make good decisions. They must be allowed the opportunity to go on extensive visits to proposed localities. There must be numerous meetings with several potential overseas partners, an extensive training program must be developed, and there must be an ongoing focus on managing the venture.

What Functions Should Be Offshored?

In Chapter 2, I introduced customer experience as a dilemma for the company that wants to outsource its customer service to a country where labor costs are lower. The reason was that customer experience is culturally determined. At this point, I want to take this rationale one step further. Let's investigate specific product or service categories and the level of service needed to satisfy their customer base. (This information is summarized in the Product–Service Decision Table on page 133.) Please realize that in the balance of this discussion, *product* refers interchangeably to either product or service.

If your product demands a perfect customer experience, then you may not want to outsource customer service to a location that is culturally distant from your customers. Industries that fall into this category are high-end services, such as financial advice, or anything that involves anticipating the customer's needs. It is simply too difficult to train and script agents who are culturally distant to provide this level of service. I did not say impossible. It is *possible* to create very good service across borders and time zones. It is just harder to create that incredible customer experience.

The next category to consider includes industries that are price sensitive, meaning margins are lower and there are substitute products readily available. This includes normal consumer goods, such as computers and software. This segment requires a delicate balance. You must offer solid customer service without impacting your ability to offer a competitive price. This is the segment that presents the greatest challenge and the greatest opportunity of great reward through outsourcing. This is the sweet spot of possibilities, where excellent decisions and impeccable execution can have a huge impact on your bottom line.

The last category is characterized by high price sensitivity and little opportunity for product differentiation. Take long distance service, for example. Consumers care mainly about price. We know the phone is going to work, and we want to talk as long as possible without worrying about the cost. Do we care how good the customer service is when we call the long distance service provider? Sure, but we will live with it if the price is low.

There will always be exceptions and disagreement in the outsourcing discussion. A June 2004 article in *Consumer Reports* published the results of a fairly extensive survey of American consumers' attitudes toward computer customer support (Computers: New Considerations 2004). Of those survey respondents who had called technical support in the last sixteen months, 28 percent reported that there were communication problems. The article blamed the communication problems on outsourcing the customer support to function. Here is the real kicker. The editors emphasized customer support as the main difference between companies, since the computers all performed quite well from a purely technical point of view. Then the article

PRODUCT–SERVICE DECISION TABLE

If your business is	Such as	Then
Price insensitive	High-end services such as financial advice	Aim to create a dynamic customer experience using in-culture agents
Highly dependent on repeat customers	Exclusive luxury goods	Consider providing in-house customer service or control vendors tightly
Price sensitive	Normal consumer goods such as computers	Aim to create a normal, positive experience free of conflict or delays
High-volume items		Consider outsourcing to reputable overseas vendors
Moderate differentiation	Control vendors tightly	Consider blended approaches and innovations to improve service and lower cost
Highly price sensitive	High-volume consumer items such as phone service	Consider outsourcing at the lowest cost
Not reliant on repeat customers	Necessities	Consider blended approaches and technological innovation to reduce cost
Little product differentiation		

proceeded to recommend only those brands that scored highly in customer support. I still believe computer support is the type of industry that lends itself well to offshoring. But the competitive pressures to lower price have to be balanced against the need to provide good service. The answer probably lies in just doing a better job to ensure that the overseas agents are providing acceptable service.

Ambiguities in Cultural Variables

One of the problems in trying to create a clear decision matrix for analyzing where to locate your call center is that groups that appear culturally similar may not necessarily be good candidates to provide customer support for each other. If the only variable to consider was language, for example, we might draw a straight line from French customers to French Canadian agents. However, this may or may not be a good idea in reality, despite the fact that they share language, cultural traits, and history. The French customer will immediately recognize the origin of the accent and might be distracted by it. You would have to conduct a focus group of your particular customer segment and draw some conclusions about whether the match is a good idea.

Contrast this with routing calls from Great Britain to Jamaica or another English-speaking Caribbean call center. British customers tend to find the Caribbean accent closer to their own version of English than American pronunciation. The island twist is usually perceived as quaint—not negative as in the French example.

Using only cultural distance to determine call center location would not have been enough in these cases. What is one to make of this? There is one characteristic of high-context cultures that makes it particularly difficult to route calls between two high-context groups: they make strong distinctions between who belongs to the group and who does not. Take the French example. Both parties shared the same language and similar culture. Yet, since the French make strong distinctions based on accent, rank, and class, it is difficult for some French customers to take Canadian or Belgian agents seriously. The emphasis is on *some* here. Most French people are not going to hang up or have a problem with a different accent. Yet, what if even a few percent of your French customers did have a problem with it? Would that be acceptable? Possibly not. Depending on the makeup of your industry and your customer profile, even a few turned-off customers may be too many. We will discuss more about French language customer service options in Chapter 10.

In our British–Jamaican scenario, the assumption is that the Jamaican agent is providing customer service to the British customer. What makes it possible to let the Jamaican agent handle the call is that the British customer tends not to have negative preconceived notions about the accent encountered. Jamaican agents can be trained not to use local slang, to simplify the accent, to slow down, and to learn about particular phrases that are different in Britain. It would be impossible to train French Canadian agents to absolutely, completely neutralize their accent and everything else that identifies them as Canadian.

The concept of customer service involves putting customers in contact with someone who can help resolve an issue or problem. It used to be that a problem required either the telephone or a walk-in situation. Now, we have e-mail and Web sites that allow chat—hence, the evolving concept of the customer contact center. The variety of customer interaction options and the fact that technology allows you to connect any customer set with any agent group anywhere in the world changes the decision-making process for where your agents should be located and what they should be doing.

The variables you should take into account in making this decision include

- customer profile (preference for type of interaction)
- customer footprint (geographic dispersion and population size)
- customer language(s)
- anticipated call volume for each geographic area
- technology availability in terms of telephony and data centers
- employee skill level, cost, and availability
- political risk
- your budget.

Following the Sun

Following the sun is a popular phrase that refers to the ability to make available support services around the world, twenty-four hours a day, seven days a week. The challenge in making this a reality is matching up the appropriate customer service language group with your customer base while creating as few customer support centers as possible in order to maintain economies of scale. This is a challenge for most large- and medium-sized businesses with international operations.

If your customer base is geographically dispersed but generally comfortable with speaking English, this is less of a challenge, since there are suitable locations evenly spread across the globe from Europe, to Singapore, to South Africa, to Australia, to North America. Many business-to-business high-tech services can operate this way. Global consumer products companies can never assume every customer speaks English. They have to consider all their markets and match the call center capacity to their customer footprint. If the scale of your operation is relatively small, your best option may be to locate your call centers in several major metropolitan areas where there are labor pools available with multiple language skills. Most major metropolitan areas in the world will have labor with skills in English, Chinese, Spanish, Arabic, French, and most other major languages. Then you can schedule your shifts and distribute your calls to get a language match that is as close to perfect as possible. Generally speaking, this approach will be more costly per call because it is more expensive to operate in major metropolitan areas in terms of both facilities and labor.

In researching this section, I set out to find a world map of language distribution. I wanted to show the geographic distribution of languages as a way to begin to think about following the sun for customer service coverage around the clock. As it turns out, there is no such thing and so I set off to create my own.

Luckily, I stumbled upon a valuable tool called worldtimezone.com, to which I give a resounding endorsement. This tool allows you to literally follow the sun live, every day, every minute of the day. I accessed the site at

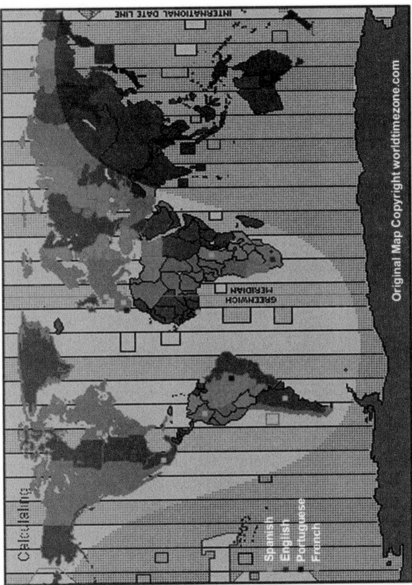

about 10:30 AM eastern standard time. The Web site image captured here reflects what parts of the globe are covered in daylight and what parts are in darkness at exactly that time. The illustration is an excellent high-level starting point for thinking about routing options based on location, time, and

even cultural distance. An English-only scenario could be South Carolina, Ireland, and Singapore, each six to eight time zones apart evenly spread across the globe. Alternatively, you could eliminate the presence in Ireland. South Carolina and Singapore are twelve time zones apart, so the difference could be compensated for by using overlapping shifts. There are any number of options, limited only by how willing you are to research and study all the locations, most of which are eager to welcome your call center. As your read about cultural characteristics in the chapters to come, keep this high-level operational perspective in mind. If you are running a 24/7 operation in one location, and serving customers across the globe, this illustration helps you anticipate what customer segments will start to call you at what time. In the illustration, customers in California are just beginning to arrive at work. Customers in Europe are reaching the end of their business day, and customers in many parts of Asia are sound asleep.

How to Use Part III

What follows in the next four chapters is an overview of some major language and cultural groups. My goal is to reveal how their cultural variables might impact where you locate your call center and how they might impact the service your customers will experience. We will also look at what people in different areas of the world like to talk about and what they don't like to talk about. In Chapter 2 we discussed the universal need to belong and the universal positive response felt when others are interested in who we are. Knowing even a few facts about a country—and by extension its customers and agents—is better than knowing nothing at all. And certainly the more you know the better. Even in brief call center exchanges, knowing something about the person you are talking to creates empathy. Agents who feel empathy are more likely to listen carefully to the person on the other end and be more interested in actually understanding what that person is telling them. Empathy motivates agents to apply reflective listening techniques, not just because they have been trained to do so, but out of a natural human instinct to want to understand.

Knowing something about another person's culture also makes it easier to strike up a conversation. For example, rushing is an American trait that is problematic for many other cultures.

> An American agent was trained to understand that people in the U.K. often do not like the rushed, results-oriented American approach to resolving issues. The agent also learned that people in the U.K. like to talk about the weather. It is a cliché, but it is true. This particular agent had been experiencing poor responses from her U.K. counterparts in working internal ticket issues. She was told to slow down the pace of the interaction and ask about the weather before getting down to business. The results were fabulous. The tension was gone, and the U.K. agents started following through on the issues. The actual phone session probably took a little longer than before, but the bottom line is that the issues were resolved faster.

Geography is particularly important when looking at culture. Mountain people are different than those living on plains. Mountain people tend to be rugged and independent. Think of Afghanistan, a very mountainous country, where staunchly independent factions have been feuding for generations. Does that mean that people living in plains are plain? No, probably not plain, but perhaps a little bit more patient in their outlook. It takes farmers a long time to work the fields of a fertile delta or for a nomadic desert tribe to walk from one oasis to the next.

The Scandinavian countries and Russia are located very far north, where winters are long and daylight is a scarce commodity during those long, cold winters. They both have vast pine forests spanning rocky terrain with creeks, rivers, and lakes cutting through the landscape. Perhaps it is not coincidental that they tend to be a little gloomy in their outlook. Russian and Scandinavian folk music is often in minor key. They tell stories about what goes on out there in the dark forests, depicting trolls and even the devil himself.

Economic conditions are important as well. A link can certainly be made between American optimism and the vast resources encountered upon arrival in the new world. In places where resources are scarce, the outlook becomes more pessimistic, perhaps even fatalistic. Most of the countries in this list are modern, wealthy nations. However, many have experienced extreme economic hardship in their history, creating scars that may linger to this day. Fatalism does not grow just out of economic hardship, however. More often, it is rooted in religion—a sense that ultimate fate is in the hands of God and that we therefore have lost some level of control over the world around us.

Before we continue this discussion I would like to add my own disclaimer. In these next chapters you may feel I am a bit overly dramatic or even simplistic at times, and I freely admit in advance to both. In reality I am in no way claiming that any national group is completely uniform and homogenous, although it may appear at times that I am doing just that. What I *am* trying to do is reflect some widespread impressions about various groups in order to provide you with some glimmers of understanding about how intercultural differences can impact your operations.

You may want to start by reading about your own country. This is likely to stir you up a little bit, meaning you may have strong opinions about what I write about you and your kin. You might agree and get a chuckle out of it; or you might disagree strongly and thus feel a rush of irritation come over you. Sometimes this negative reaction occurs because a generalization hits you close to home, so to speak. In other words, you may not be very comfortable being associated with one of the common traits in your culture. An example of this would be a German who is not comfortable being associated with the German obsession with punctuality. Saying that Germans are obsessed with punctuality may seem like an inference that Germans are somehow robot-like—an unattractive trait for a German who is more nonconformist or creative.

When you get to those sections to which you have a strong reaction, please offer your perspective by posting a message in the book blog. (This is explained in the Author's Note on page 8.) Keep in mind that I am well aware that there are wide varieties of perspectives and behaviors within every culture and between individuals. You are learning about some preconceived notions that others might have made about you and other people in your culture. These notions often present obstacles in our interaction, so being aware is going to be very helpful.

Not every country and culture is examined in depth here. Perhaps European cultures are overrepresented both quantitatively and qualitatively, which is somewhat a reflection on my personal experience in those cultures. Much of the value in this section is in asking the key questions; the model of one country can be applied to others. With this in mind, I invite you to supplement these readings with your insights by participating in the online book blog.

 TRAINING ACTIVITY: Learning About Culture

Select a country and ask your group to write down two descriptive words or phrases about the country you are about to discuss. Go around the room and ask them to share their words or phrases. Write down what they say on a board. Either discuss each item as you write it, or write them all down and then go back and discuss the entire list. As moderator, either validate what they say or perhaps temper their perceptions with added insight. Avoid characterizing their input as right or wrong. Instead emphasize the differences in perception that will become apparent as the list develops. If possible, include in the discussion an elaboration of the impression each participant intended to convey; it may be entirely different from what they actually communicated. Understanding the differences between definition and connotation may reduce frustration in these interactions.

8

English-Language Customer Service

English is the lingua franca of business. English is also the principle language of the largest pool of customers who need support via some kind of contact center infrastructure. Think about it: Australia, Canada, India, the United Kingdom, Ireland, the United States, New Zealand, Jamaica, Singapore, the Philippines, and several African countries including South Africa, all use English as their primary language in international business interactions. Add to that all the people around the world who have learned English in school, and it is easy to understand why the ability to speak English is a valuable asset throughout the call center industry.

But English is not a uniform and homogenous language that is spoken and written the same way everywhere. Far from it. The dialects, the slang, the cadence, the humor, the idioms, and the general vocabulary that are applied to express everyday events and feelings vary widely as the language reaches across the globe. From the earthy Irish, to the cropped London cockney, to the expressive Jamaican, to the drawn-out American South, and to the singsong of Indian English, it is no wonder that clear communication becomes an issue. In fact, the main problem is often not getting the agent to speak clearly but rather having the agent understand what the customer is saying. Perhaps it would not be such a bad idea to program the ACD to provide the following message after the obligatory "this call may be recorded" notice: "Because the person you will speak with may speak a version of English that is very different from your own, you are encouraged to slow down your speech and avoid the use of slang."

Relax, that was a tongue-in-cheek recommendation. In the rest of this chapter I will discuss a bit of the background of some of the more prominent English-language sites: India, Ireland, the United Kingdom, the United States, Canada, and Australia. I have put Singapore in the Asia section, simply because from a Westerner's perspective Singapore stands out primarily as a bridge into China and the rest of Asia. In any case, not all English language call center options are included. For example, the Philippines, which is rapidly emerging as a truly attractive option, is not covered in detail. What is interesting about the Filipinos is that they are probably closer to the United States culturally than India is. The U.S. military presence on the islands, which officially ended several years ago, has meant that Americans and Filipinos have already learned how to work together. Labor is plentiful, and the required infrastructure is available in major metropolitan areas.

Because English reaches every corner of the world, it is particularly important to be open-minded when considering call center options. Who would have thought a few years ago that India and the Philippines would be such dominant forces in the industry? Now, South Africa is rapidly emerging as a great way to augment your English-language footprint around the world. There are call centers in Johannesburg and in Cape Town. South African call center companies are traveling around the world to attract your business. And, why not? They speak English, they have the technology, and they have the workforce to accomplish it.

Do not forget about the other English-speaking countries in Africa that are trying to emulate South Africa. We have already mentioned Ghana, but there is also Uganda, which has undergone economic liberalization and deregulation in the telecommunications sector. Kampala would be the most likely destination as it is a rapidly growing urban area with educated workers, high unemployment and annual salaries of around $4,000.00. One might think that Nairobi, Kenya, would be another possible destination where English is spoken and there is a decent supply of skilled labor. Kenya's telephone infrastructure is not really up to par, however, and, whether real or not, the country suffers from a reputation of rampant corruption. Africa will be a market to watch in the coming years, nevertheless.

India

Indian civilization is one of the oldest in the world, dating back at least five thousand years. Aryan occupation created a merger with the earlier inhabitants to form the classical Indian culture that we know today. If you like art, compare Indian and Persian miniature paintings to see how these cultures have influenced each other. Arab and Turkish incursions were followed by European traders beginning in the late fifteenth century. By the nineteenth century, Britain had assumed political control of virtually all Indian lands. India gained independence from Great Britain in 1947. In 1971, India was divided into the secular state of India and the Muslim state of Pakistan (*World Fact Book* 2002).

India's economy is made up of agriculture, handicrafts, a wide range of modern industries, and a multitude of support services. Reforms to encourage foreign investment and privatization of domestic industry have resulted in good economic growth. Despite the widely recognized success of Atal Bihari Vajpayii's BJP party's economic policies, the Congress Party, under the leadership of Italian-born Sonia Gahhi, won the 2004 election on a platform that catered to the rural poor.

While Hindi is the national language and primary tongue of a third of the population, English is the most important language for national, political, and commercial communication. In addition, there are fourteen other official languages spoken in local provinces.

When it comes to telephony, two separate worlds exist. Few people have telephones at home, and there is a long waiting list to get phone service. However, there is mobile phone service in urban areas. Major cities such as Bangalore, Bombay, and New Delhi offer a strong infrastructure of submarine cables that provide the backbone for the call center, software, and data services industries. In poor rural areas, there is a shortage of landlines, and wireless service can be spotty.

India: Cultural Analysis

In some ways, it is ridiculous to try to identify a single national character in a country with over one billion people, multiple religions, and over three hundred languages. However, there are some appropriate generalities. Indians are generally less hurried than Westerners. Being idle is indeed seen as virtue due to commonly held religious beliefs. Life for Indians evolves in stages from childhood, youth, working age, and then to old age. Each stage has its own perspective and life must be allowed to unfold without resistance and interference. Indians are also a feeling people. They are in tune with their feelings and the beliefs that underlie them. You will have better success with them if you are in tune with this perspective and refrain from referring solely to facts and project deadlines.

India is, in general, a poor nation. However, the India that you are likely to encounter in setting up call center operations will be very different from what you saw reading *National Geographic* twenty years ago. Just as in Mexico and other developing countries, there is a sizable educated middle class. Though discrimination based on caste is illegal, the inequality in the social structure is still a reflection of those deeply held beliefs. As an outsider, it is difficult to read subtle communications and perceptions in daily interaction from one caste to another. It helps to understand that from the perspective of the individual, caste identification can be a source of comfort because the individual knows where he belongs. That lack of anxiety has a disarming quality, which I find very attractive. Among high-caste members, a strongly ingrained sense of superiority can cause problems when encountering individuals from cultures where status is achieved instead of inherited. It can cause conflict on an external level as the Indian can be perceived as a high-brow as opposed to a peer. Internally, for Indians abroad, it can cause angst on an individual level, as they are no longer steeped in the reverence they are accustomed to.

Much of learning and education in India takes place through rote memorization. Widely held group beliefs are reinforced in this manner. The result, as it is in many other high-context cultures, is that you are unlikely to change their opinion on a given subject just by presenting facts as one might in the West. This will be less of a factor when dealing with the Indian middle class, who are more likely to have been exposed to abstract, analytical methods of learning.

Paul Davies, author of *What's This India Business?* and an expert on doing business in India, says that accountability can be an issue with Indian workers (Davies 2004). If you notice this, perhaps it is because in the Indian culture decision making and general responsibility rest completely with the person in charge. People who are not in charge are reluctant to take on that role because of the heavy burdens that come with it. Further, religious and cultural beliefs allow *general circumstance* as an acceptable excuse for things not getting done, a trait similar to the fatalism described for other cultures.

India: Communication Style

It takes from one to two months to train a college-educated Indian to handle calls with an acceptable accent and speech pattern. This involves taking on an interaction style that ranges from a lively give-and-take to a more matter-of-fact exchange of information. The level of effort that some companies have put into neutralizing agent accents is simply amazing. I know of one company that applied what managers called a *six-sigma approach*, loosely meaning they approached the problem scientifically from several angles to ensure a holistic solution. This process included focus groups, validation with language experts, trial training programs, and customer surveys to ensure the experience was acceptable. While there are organizations, such as Convergys, Wipro, and a host of smaller consulting services, who officially provide this service, I also suspect that there is a covert element as to how this is being done. There is not a whole lot of public relations mileage in bragging about how one neutralizes an accent by applying the most modern training and management techniques. Customers don't want to feel they are being tricked into feeling comfortable with your customer service department.

In *What's This India Business?*, Davies describes his encounter with an Indian call center. I admit I feel some measure of relief that this particular agent had not completely changed his communication style:

> One aspect I noticed when watching an agent in a call center was that as it is the telephone voice that is important, the body language is unaffected and remains Indian. It is absolutely fascinating to listen to a rather refined English accent while watching hands moving and the head rolling in a typical Indian way (Davies 2004).

It is probably a good thing that most customer service conducted between India and the West is over the telephone. There are many Indian unwritten rules and nonverbal cues that contradict Western nonverbal cues. Here are just a few:

- In India, nodding up and down means yes, while nodding side to side can mean no or that you are listening. Just think of the misunderstandings those visuals could cause.
- The shoe is considered very dirty, so you must be careful what you do with your feet. I once saw an Indian ambassador interviewed on television. The anchor had nonchalantly crossed his legs with the bottom of his shoe pointed right into the face of the ambassador. The ambassador was twisting in disgust, holding his head back while looking down at the shoe over his nose.
- When interacting with an Indian, remember that the Indian concepts of time and urgency have different rules compared to the West. *Allowing* is a key concept. Things will just take slightly longer. Allow people to finish what they are saying. Allow the conversation to go where someone wants to take it. When on the telephone, learn from the pace and ceremony of the traditional *namaste* greeting of putting your palms together in front of you while bowing. Add a measure of sincerity and pause slightly to ensure that the greeting is not rushed. This practice gives face. Participate in small talk, maybe about sports or events in the news.
- Use formal address and be aware of the person's rank. If you need decisions to be made, realize ahead of time that you may need to go higher in the organization to get what you want.

Ireland

The failed 1916 Easter Monday Rebellion touched off several years of guerrilla warfare that in 1921 resulted in independence from the United Kingdom for the twenty-six southern counties, while the six northern counties remained part of Great Britain. In 1948 Ireland withdrew from the British commonwealth. It joined the European community in 1973. Irish governments have sought the peaceful unification of Ireland and have cooperated with Britain against terrorist groups. A peace settlement for Northern Ireland, approved in 1998, was implemented the following year (*World Fact Book* 2002).

Ireland has a modern, trade-dependent economy. Agriculture, once the most important sector, is now dwarfed by industry. Although exports remain the primary engine for Ireland's robust growth, the economy is also benefiting from a rise in consumer spending and recovery in both construction and business investment.

The list of companies that have located their call centers in Ireland reads like a who's who of business: IBM, American Airlines, Gateway, Compaq, and UPS to name a few. The only problem now is this gem has been discovered, and labor availability and cost are issues that you must explore carefully before making a decision to locate in Ireland. Such are the laws of supply and demand. Once everyone realized the wonderful qualities of the Irish workforce, demand went up, and supply could not keep up. Companies compete for talent, wages go up, other related costs go up, and eventually things will balance out. I think everyone agrees that Ireland is still a great choice.

Ireland: Cultural Analysis

First of all, the Irish are not British, and you must never confuse the two or make generalizations that lump the Irish in with the other peoples in the British Isles. In fact, the Irish make it a point to reject cultural traits that they interpret as British elitism, sarcasm, and excessive reliance on rules, to name a few. Further, they are obsessed with expressing their separate cultural identity through art, literature, music and storytelling. It would be fair to describe the Irish as more high context than the Britishs, Scots, and Welsh.

They identify strongly with their local village and evaluate the world though its collective beliefs. The Irish may appear cliquish as they distinguish strongly between members and nonmembers of various groups. Perhaps although the Irish do not realize it themselves, this is often interpreted by foreigners as reserved snobbishness. That said, the Irish *do* share several traits with their island neighbors. They are traditional, they enjoy a healthy discussion, and they believe in fair play. These traits, mixed with strong connections to North America and rapid social and economic development, make for a rich combination of local engagement and global perspective.

The social fabric of Ireland has undergone tremendous strain over the years—war, poverty, massive emigration, urbanization, and in recent years, extremely rapid economic development. The general health of the Irish at home and abroad is a testament to the strength of the Irish family. Their ability to maintain their common bonds at home and around the world draws universal admiration. Their success in maintaining their identity in the face of change and persecution can be compared to the Jewish experience.

The educational system of Ireland is second to none. A highly skilled labor force has allowed Ireland to attract many large high-tech companies to set up operations there. Being a small country, opportunities are sometimes limited in some fields. It is therefore not uncommon to see the Irish plying their craft around the world in North America, Australia, and the rest of Europe.

Ireland: Communication Style

Irish interaction provides many clues as to how they might be classified as more high-context than their neighbors. One must listen carefully to Irish conversation, for the true meaning is often implied rather than stated outright. Like the French, who are more high-context than most of Europe, the Irish value wit, favor eloquence of expression, and can be animated in their presentation. Add to that their love for poetry, storytelling, and music, and you get some of the liveliest interaction humanly possible. Pay attention, participate, and don't leave the conversation hanging as this can make them feel both disappointed and uncomfortable.

When interacting with the Irish, be yourself. It's fine to be authentic and rustic, but not crude. Give some indication that you are lively. Use formal address but show some feelings. Don't be snobbish or distant. Telling a good story is sure to go over well. Storytelling is rarely encouraged in the call center setting, but if you are looking to establish some rapport, this would be one strategy for creating a bond with the Irish.

Another high-context trait is that the Irish do not like to say no, so you will have to listen for it carefully. This is really no different than other cultures that have the same trait. As if that was not tricky enough, be aware of the charm of the Irish because they've got it and they will use it. They will tell you stories, stringing you along and making you believe that the price of tea in China is going to affect us all in a really big way. In other words, don't believe everything they tell you. While the truth can be stretched for effect, it is rarely with any malicious intent.

Popular conversational topics would include Irish authors such as Joyce and Shaw. This is sure to flatter any Irish person. Throw in some Irish poetry or heroic legends and you will have a friend.

United Kingdom

At its height, the British Empire covered one quarter of the earth's surface, and the sun shone on it twenty-four hours a day. As the physical control of the empire gradually diminished, the United Kingdom still remained and remains an economic power, particularly in services such as publishing, insurance, and financial services. The U.K. economy is diverse, including natural resources such as oil and gas, medical research and manufacturing. The Manchester region has a thriving call center industry. The city has a huge labor pool of qualified workers.

The islands that make up the United Kingdom are located in western Europe between the Atlantic Ocean and the North Sea. The climate is temperate, as the moisture of the Gulf Stream steadily rolls in across the Atlantic from the Gulf of Mexico.

United Kingdom: Cultural Analysis

We all harbor several stereotypes about the British: the stiffness of the Queen and the royal family, the suave James Bond, the boyish Paul McCartney. If you look closely at these stereotypes, you will notice some common traits, and if you are British you may take issue with me. Beneath an apparently very controlled surface lies a person who executes with crushing efficiency. Consciously or unconsciously, I think we all find this contradiction intriguing. The Queen, who really looks like a school teacher, owns the most brilliant jewelry and lives in the most fabulous castles. James Bond inspires trust but would stab you in the back for his cause. Paul McCartney looks and speaks like a choir boy, but his music is so brilliant that it would have you cry one moment and scream for joy the next. This character of contradiction also offers a metaphor for their communication style, which is understated with hidden meanings and sharp irony.

Britain's past as a world empire (plus the continued Anglo-Saxon cultural hegemony through the United States) often still colors the individual's outlook. That outlook is one of being the originator, carrying a certain paternal sense of responsibility for Western civilization.

United Kingdom: Communication Style

The British are great communicators in every sense. They often speak well, argue clearly, listen attentively, and provide quality feedback. They also write, and so should you in establishing relationships with the British — write thank-you notes, summarize meetings, and so on. Foreigners have to listen for subtle, hidden meaning in everything the British say. British sitcoms offer great insight into their conversational style — dry, understated, stoic, and ironic.

While it is not an outright insult for a foreigner to use the term "English" as a blanket description that includes Scots and Welsh, they would prefer that we have a better appreciation for their unique histories and traditions. So it is a good idea to learn to differentiate if you are going to interact a lot with them often.

It may sound trite, but the British do indeed like to talk about the weather. Just a quick mention expresses a show of concern about how things are where they are. It is about having a sense of place and concern about their comfort. It is human, and it is light, so just try it with them and see whether business flows just a little more easily when there is a mutual awareness about the weather.

It is a good idea not to add unnecessary drama to situations. Getting emotional about issues is seen as weakness. Remember that the British are not afraid of a healthy argument, so don't get them started. They may seem calm on the surface, and this could manifest itself in several ways. Sometimes it may feel as if there is a lack of urgency, especially to Americans. Sometimes, you may finish an exchange, and yet there has been no decision made for future action. Do not force the issue but instead schedule a follow-up to discuss it further. Lastly, as tempting as it may be, it is definitely not a good idea to imitate their dialects. They will not get insulted, but you will look like a fool.

United States

The world still sees the United States as a young country. But it was truly the world's first modern democracy when it adopted its constitution in 1789. Emerging from the trauma of a horrific civil war in 1865 and an economic catastrophe known as the Great Depression in the 1930s, the United States reigns as the economic, political, and military superpower in the world (*World Fact Book* 2002). The historically white Christian population is rapidly transforming into a tapestry of white, black, Latino, and Asian people, with representations from every nook and cranny on the planet. From the Atlantic to the Pacific Oceans, terrain and climate vary from lush coastal areas, fertile deltas, arid desert, paradise tropics, and hellish cold plains. The United States is the birthplace of the telephone, the computer, and the software that drives the call center industry today.

United States: Cultural Analysis
Because of the variety of ethnic groups that make up the American character, it is difficult to make generalizations. There are multiple subcultures such as African-American, Italian-American, and numerous others. Still the core of the American character is northern European, Anglo-Saxon, with a strong Puritan influence. This cultural core is strong enough that some cross-cultural experts go so far as to say that the myth of the melting pot is nothing more than that—a myth (Weaver 1988). Conformity to a complex mixture of Puritanism and individualism, as defined by achievement, exert tremendous pressures on both immigrants and youth. Americans are positive, friendly, creative, informal and future oriented.

On Hofstede's collectivist/individualist scale, the United States ranked as the most individualistic culture, one point ahead of Australia (Hofstede

1997). Freedom and equality of individual opportunity shapes the social structure. Visitors are often struck by extreme contrasts in material wealth — a brutal, yet accepted consequence of equal opportunity.

Status is achieved. Sayings such as "You are what you do" or "You are what you drive" reflect how identity is obtained. This drive for status means that Americans work a lot, often taking just two weeks vacation per year or even less.

American children are taught to dream, to believe. The frontier spirit is still alive and well. Youths are encouraged to explore their talents and creativity. The education system is one of second chances. It is never too late to change direction or, if necessary, start over. Dropouts return and finish high school at an adult age. Retirees return to college. Doctors change careers and become lawyers. Such educational opportunity and mobility is unavailable or at least unrealistic in most other countries.

United States: Communication Style
Americans are obsessed with written contracts. Seeing is believing. Ink on paper is something tangible and real. Because of the mobility in American society, group affiliations are loose, and friendships are sincere, yet may be based on mutual benefit. Americans generally make good listeners. They express their opinion, and they want to hear yours. Social distance and nonverbal communication depends on cultural subgroup, with people of Anglican heritage being less animated than Italian-Americans, for example.

While this may seem too obvious and even cause for dismissal in the call center, resist at all costs the urge to moralize about the ills of American society. You won't hurt feelings, but you will be ignored and appear uninformed, so you will completely lose credibility.

Some people believe the tacky aspects of American popular culture constitutes a lack of "culture" in a traditional sense on the part of Americans. This is a very dangerous assumption to make. The level of sophistication may be uneven, but if you harbor thoughts like that about Americans, you are indeed the one who is misinformed. If in a customer service situation you need to offer historical context and information that seems obvious to you, do not talk down to them. Instead, draw them in with your storytelling and your enthusiasm.

Americans are results oriented with the main goal being profit. They want to see the bottom line right away. "What is the point?" "What is in it for us?" Make your points obvious and even repeat them a few times for clarity. In business situations, consider that your American counterparts are accountable right now. Did you understand that? In a very real, tangible, I-am-going-to-get-fired-if-you-can't-help-me-with-this-right-now kind of way, the American must see results. As difficult as it may be for you, whether you are in India or in the United Kingdom, try to empathize with that situation for a moment. Demonstrate an appreciation for that, and you will have fully heard your American counterpart. It will diffuse the tension, because now the American feels that he has an ally.

Canada

It may be tempting to just skip Canada and say that its culture is similar to American culture. True, there are many similarities. Both were settled at same time by similar groups of people. English is the most common language, though French is also spoken. The Anglican heritage also means many values are similar across the countries.

Canada is slightly more feminine than the United States, as exemplified by more progressive social policies. Canadians are also very secure in their identity. A recent beer commercial depicts a young man on stage going on in a frantic monologue about how he is Canadian, not an American. The popularity of this commercial might make you think this would indicate a certain level of identity crisis. On the contrary, because Canadians are so clear about their own identity, they are frustrated with the rest of the world not being able to differentiate them from their neighbor to the south.

So what is this Canadian identity, and what makes it different from the pervasive American culture that is also part of their everyday live? The astute visitor to Canadian cities can sense a difference in atmosphere. The electricity and danger of "anything is possible" that one feels in New York or Detroit is gone. It is replaced with a much more casual stride combined with a certain flair and ease, not just in French-speaking cities of Québec and Montreal, but also in Toronto and elsewhere.

What does this mean for customer service skills in call centers? Mostly that it is important to know that Canadians are not Americans and that Canadians are not insecure about it, but they know that they are different and they want you to know that they are different. Perhaps the best way to do this is to acknowledge your awareness of the customer being Canadian as opposed to American. Instruct agents to simply say "I see you are located in Vancouver, Canada. Very nice!" That will suffice as a recognition that you know Vancouver is not a suburb of Seattle. It is just amazing how carefully selected statements like that can make a world of difference in making people feel comfortable and understood.

Australia

Australians have a streak in their character that stems from the fact that many early settlers did not go there of their own free will. Regardless of how or why settlers arrived, they encountered a landscape that was much more challenging than the American land of plenty. Take a look at an Australian map, and you will find names such as Lake Disappointment, Cape Catastrophe, and Disaster Bay. For the same reasons that Americans are friendly and outgoing, Australians are likewise. The challenges they faced in building modern Australia have made them different, and it is very difficult to put your finger on exactly how. The answer might be found in their humor, which is often rooted in superhuman acts to overcome nature's challenges. The film *Crocodile Dundee* entertains us with their heroics and their tales. The truth below that humor, of course, is countless tragedies where nature won out over human heroics.

As far as what this means for customer service, be careful about interpreting the implications. While there is perhaps a sense that there is nothing you can throw at Australians that they cannot overcome and a light-heartedness— that things are not so bad after all—these do not give you a license to treat Australians casually. I find that cultures that we think of as rich in traditions of humor, including Irish and Australian, can be the trickiest to engage on that level. Humor is almost always high-context in nature, evoking hidden meanings that provide comfort when shared. But you and I have not really experienced the context being evoked, have we? If we show some level of respect and reverence for their experience, we are more likely to build connections that are meaningful in the customer service setting than if we artificially try to mimic their quick wit.

9

Spanish-Language Customer Service

There are intricacies as to how the Spanish language has evolved in Spain, South America, and Central America and how those variations are perceived from one Spanish speaker to the next. That is the first and most general statement that can be made on this topic. I have heard statements such as Costa Rican Spanish is even better than Castilian because it is more like the original Spanish of the conquistadors. Or that Puerto Rican Spanish is more colloquial than many others. Or that Chilean Spanish tends to be a good mainstream form of Spanish. Those statements do not necessarily help me as a non-Spanish speaker decide how to route calls, as they are probably examples of perception rather than reality. Beyond that, all Spanish speakers are passionate about their language. The language itself is so tightly and intricately tied to their culture. That means any discussion about who should talk to who in the call center should best be handled by Spanish speakers on a case-by-case basis depending on your customer profile.

In the end, Spanish speakers understand each other quite well. There is a great deal of travel between these countries, satellite television shows are broadcast across the Spanish-speaking world, and even musical performers are enjoyed across borders. Therefore, accents should not be a huge issue. If it is, accent neutralization training is available for Spanish agents just as it is for English speakers. From what I understand, accent neutralization works better for Spanish speakers than for English speakers. That is probably because as a whole, Spanish speakers are culturally closer to one another than, let's say, Americans and Indians.

There are some interesting cultural nuances that must be emphasized. Mexican culture is covered in a separate section below. Island nations such as Puerto Rico and Cuba have some interesting traits that make them a little different. For some reason, they tend to be more direct in their approach. With Cubans, I would dare to even say that they are almost low-context in their interactions, with a more probing and factual style. There may be a need for coaching in this area, but if you are running a Spanish-language call center, you will be able to have honest conversations about communication style with your team. In general, Spanish speakers use language to convey class and authority. Much like the French, eloquence is an art form that not everyone can attain. And listeners can hear it.

American Spanish speakers, in particular, are so used to hearing a variety of dialects that there should be little opportunity to either surprise or offend. On the other hand, a customer who is in Peru, for example, is likely to want to speak to a Peruvian. This should not come as a surprise to anyone. I challenge you right now to say who you would expect to speak to on the other side. Do you not expect an in-country accent? Why shouldn't you? It seems rather natural and obvious. If you are running an all-Americas call center in the United States, you could deliberately staff your center with a variety of nationalities and do skill-based routing based on country-of-origin detection on the ACD.

What follows is a closer examination of cultures of Mexico and Spain. For outsiders, these treatments offer some insights into all of Spanish culture. Indeed, these two are in some ways the polar opposites of the Spanish world, with other Spanish cultures as nuances between these two. For Spanish speakers who are reading this as an exercise in self-discovery, please remember that the traits are described from an outsider's point of view. Step back and look at my perceptions impassively and try to understand how misunderstandings can spring from that point of view. This is the essence of the cultural awareness that will improve our conversation.

Mexico

Mexico was ruled by Spain for over three centuries before gaining independence. Perhaps that is why Independence Day, has a very deep meaning for Mexicans. With a population of over 100 million, the terrain ranges from desert to tropical, and the elevation ranges from high plateaus to low coastal deltas. Despite a major trade agreement, improved relations with the United States, and recent elections that were widely recognized as free and fair, Mexico continues to grapple with economic problems and social inequity. Ethnically and religiously, Mexico is homogenous with 90 percent of the population being of Native American (Aztec or Mayan) origin or a mixture between Native American and Spanish (*mestiso*). Mexico is overwhelmingly Catholic.

The telephone system is modern, with mobile service available especially in urban areas. With a sizeable middle class in places such as Mexico City, there has existed a need to offer in-language customer support for any number of consumer goods and services for many years now.

It is useful to contrast European Spanish culture with the cultures that have truly integrated their Native American heritage into their national cultures in the new world. Just look at how Aztec and Mayan traditions have blended into Mexican culture or how modern Peruvian culture is rich in native traditions. Not only does the ethnic makeup reflect this blend, but words and behaviors as well. What is more, Mexicans and Peruvians identify with it. Mexicans would rather be called Mexican than Latino or Spanish or anything else. It is not that you are going to insult them; it is just imprecise, lacking a full understanding of who they are.

Mexico: Cultural Analysis

Mexican culture is changing rapidly. The values and beliefs will differ between the urban middle class, where Western business methods are influencing daily life, and people in rural areas, where tradition and continuity prevail. A recent Hofstede survey of Mexican managers found that the cultural traits had moved significantly toward the Western side of the scale, with more emphasis on individualism and an acceptance of flatter organizational models.

Family is central in Mexican life. *Family* includes extended family and close connections between extended families through business and marriage. This results in a strong sense of in-group and out-group status. Relationships are much more important than any short-term gain. What does that mean for the call center? Now that you know this, you will be better able to relate to a Mexican who in conversation makes reference to his family. If family is part of the context, then it may be time to sit up and take note, because now it is personal and it is important. In a business situation, family offers access to resources. It means that things can get done.

Mexicans are somewhat class and rank conscious. If a customer wants to speak to a manager, then accommodate him. Every call center has some procedures for escalating issues to a higher level. You may not want to pull the old trick of just forwarding the call to another agent. However, when you do this to an American, it is perfectly fine, especially if the agent next door is a little more experienced and can actually fix whatever the problem is. The American doesn't care who does the fixing, just as long as it gets done and done quickly. With the Mexican, his motivation for escalation may be different. He may have been uncomfortable discussing his issues with somebody who is his junior in every sense. Remember that rank and eloquence of expression are frequently closely knit in Latin cultures, including Mexico. So, Mexican customers might be able to detect if they have still not reached someone of their own stature.

Mexicans are receptive to new ideas. You may not always change their minds, however. Their subjective beliefs are deeply rooted and shared with their family and extended family.

Mexico: Communication Style

Mexicans are warm, hospitable, and personable. They are genuinely interested in every aspect of who you are. Therefore, building personal relationships is extremely important. In the call center setting, the ACD can be set up in such a way that good customers have a higher likelihood of talking to the same person every time they call. Even providing direct phone numbers to specific agents is acceptable in certain business environments.

Listening for the hidden "no" cannot be overemphasized. It will come out in very subtle ways. Often it is a redirection, such as "you may want to consider doing this instead" or "have you ever tried this way of getting it done?" The hidden "no" has been covered in several parts of this book, so there is no need in repeating it here.

Be aware that Mexican business people are often well informed and savvy about their situations. If you are not the same, they will interpret that as weakness. Being well informed, articulate, and neatly dressed are all part of that same preparedness. If you want to run a call center to impress Mexican customers, the agents should be well prepared and articulate. This advice seems like common sense, but sometimes the hardest thing is getting the basics right.

Spain

Tucked between France to the north and oceans to the West and south, Spain sometimes gets forgotten as a major European economy. Spain competed with England and France for world dominance in the colonial era. A devastating civil war in the years leading up to World War II pitted communist and fascist factions against each other. In modern times, Spain, like Italy, has had to play a catch-up role to keep pace with France, Germany, and the United Kingdom. With over forty million people, a vibrant economy, and a rich history, Spain teems with an unusual certainty in its sense of time and space. It is now firmly engaged in the pan-European experiment and should be thought of as modern and viable in every sense. The Barcelona region is a popular call center destination with modern infrastructure and plenty of available labor.

Spain: Cultural Analysis

Human, *romantic*, and *real* are good descriptive words for the Spaniards. While they share an affinity for style and eloquence of expression with their Latin neighbors, the Spaniards do not put on a show the way the French and Italians do. Spaniards value intuition and view the world through emotions. Their language can express emotions like no other, down to the finest nuance. One might even say that they are sensitive, and outsiders should be aware that the concept of honor plays a central role in a person's life. They have a great love of poetry and literature (as can be said for Spanish-speaking countries in Latin America). Unlike Italian humor, Spanish humor is comprised primarily of understatements and double meanings.

As a country that has seen extremely rapid economic development and urbanization in the last thirty years, Spain's social structure has changed. Group membership (neighborhood, village, and so on) still confers status, but professional success is also important. They have a strong distaste for excess and those who would flaunt it. They even see a certain dignity in poverty.

Beyond being fatalistic in their outlook (as are other Latin cultures where the Catholic Church has a strong influence), the Spaniards have unique perspective on life. Outsiders may interpret them as party animals, but it is really a deeply rooted rejection of all things related to the rat race that tends to enslave us. In Spain one must not be a slave to the appointment book and deadlines. What is truly real, what truly matters is who you *are*, your feelings and your relationships. In dealing with them, excessive emphasis on the rules of modern life can cause them to feel as if you are "dragging them down."

Spanish organizations are hierarchically structured, much as in Mexico or in France. This means you should be aware of your own status and pay attention to the organizational rank of others. This is particularly useful in call center interaction, as your caller from Spain may perceive that he or she is not dealing with someone who is of his or her own status. The best way to handle this situation is to yield to the customer's wish to talk to a manager.

Spain: Communication Style

Spaniards are less formal than Spanish speakers in Latin America. Interaction is intense. They gesture, maintain eye contact, pat each other on the back, and so on. When dealing with the Spanish, it is important to listen. They like to express themselves, so give them plenty of time and let them finish. You will make a friend if they sense that you hear them clearly. Therefore, validate what they are saying rather than present opposing arguments. This will allow you to steer the conversation in a different direction later, if needed. As with Italians, you may confide personal matters in them (if you feel comfortable doing so).

There are plenty of things not to do when interacting with the Spanish. Never rush them or force the issues. They really don't like that, and you can expect a healthy dose of what Americans call "push back." In other words, pushing will have the opposite of its intended effect. Also, do not get bogged down in details that get in the way of how you are experiencing the moment. Details can be worked out later. Say, "I will forward that to you in e-mail." Boom! Now you can continue the *real* conversation. Never patronize with facts and rules, lists of accomplishments and other artificial credentials. Who are you to judge, or be the messenger of truth?

Positive methods for speeding things up include appealing to Spaniards' emotions. This is much less dramatic and much easier to do than you might think. You might say, "I complement you on your choice. I would have chosen the same item myself." Or "The same thing happened to my mother last year. I really sympathize with you." As a contrast, when hearing customer support people say things like that, I am immediately turned off. Being half Swedish, half American, I often do not relish taking time to listen to someone's personal issues or opinions. However, trust me when I say that my impatience is not shared by most people on this planet and likely not your customers either.

10

European Cultures and Customer Service Options

I f English-language customer service is a good candidate for a global 24/7 scheme with large hubs and outsourcing, and if Spanish-language operations are likewise candidates for savings through scale and outsourcing, then Europe is a little bit trickier to classify. There is no other environment that has so many highly advanced consumer markets speaking so many languages in such a condensed area. With eastern European countries joining the European Union, things are getting even more complex. At the same time, there are more great opportunities and more options than ever.

Serving Europe will usually require some kind of hybrid model. For example, you could have a hub in a major metropolitan area such as Brussels, where you serve all the major languages: English, French, German, and Dutch. Then you could create small satellite centers in Stockholm and Prague to serve the outlying areas. These regional centers could be linked to the ACD in the main office so that you could manage all the call activities. At night, maybe you could switch all the calls to an American call center and offer English-only service or the option to leave an in-language message.

Such a strategy should work well for a while. Eventually, you might have to expand and create a French-dedicated center in France and a German dedicated center in Germany. To save money, though, you might also route all your English calls to an outsourced service in India or the Philippines, while Spanish language issues could be handled from an American outsourced service in Arizona.

I used the word *hybrid* very deliberately. In the end, all your global call center infrastructure scenarios are hybrid conglomerations of solutions that will work for a while but probably not forever. Eventually the business will grow, contract, increase, or decrease in importance. Change is the only constant you can count on. When looking at creating a European solution, this reality becomes very tangible. One way to put it is that you can't cheat when dealing with Europe. Can't you just picture an executive who needs an Asian customer service solution just waving his arm and saying "set something up in Singapore." The choice of location *seems* fairly obvious: just get it done, there is no need for debate.

Can you "just set something up" in Europe? You can if your scale is relatively small. If your business grows rapidly, however, I promise you that there will come a day when it makes no sense at all to service German customers from Brussels or French customers from Amsterdam. The moment that realization hits, you are forced to move to some kind of hybrid model.

Belgium

In many ways, Belgium is a crossroads of Europe and the world. You could think of Brussels as the Rome of modern Europe. This city functions as the center of a great, ongoing experiment to integrate the political and economic functions of individual European countries. So real and tangible is the force of integration in Belgium that many Belgians admit that their own identity shifts between their local affiliation and Europe at large.

Belgians are either of French-speaking Walloon origin to the south or of Flemish speaking origin to the north. Only about 10 percent of the population would not fall into one of these two categories, though at least 75 percent of the population is Roman Catholic (*World Fact Book* 2002). While there have been tensions between these two groups in the past, the overall European movement has served as a mitigating force. Belgium is a modern country with a diverse industrial infrastructure.

Physically, Belgium is sandwiched between the Netherlands to the north and France to the South. The weather in Belgium lacks the extremes of either heat or cold throughout the four seasons. The Gulf Stream brings rain and moisture over its coastal plains, creating excellent agricultural conditions.

Belgium is highly developed. The telephone infrastructure is modern. Modern call center infrastructure should be either available or easy to set up in any urban or suburban area. Many large international companies have located in the suburbs outside Brussels, close to the airport. This general area is attractive for companies wishing to provide in-language support across Europe because of widely available labor with language skills. This labor force does not come at low cost, however. Pessimists will add that French speakers in France and Dutch speakers in the Netherlands are not particularly fond of Belgian accents. My personal experience is that those attitudes are exaggerated. It is recommended that you conduct some customer surveys before you set your services up this way, however.

Belgium: Cultural Analysis

Because Belgium is made up of two ethnic groups with different languages, it is hard to define one national character. There are areas where one might say that the Walloons are less French than the French, and the Flemish are less Dutch than the Dutch and where Belgium as a whole has certain unique characteristics. Both loathe extravagance and aggressiveness, the Walloons a little less so (the Flemish even more so than the Dutch). Both value compromise in decision making. Both value the bottom line (in terms of money) over other forms of reward. Both are outward-looking and think of themselves as Europeans. Still, knowing about Dutch and French culture is a good starting point in understanding the Belgians.

Belgium is wealthy country. The source of wealth in the Flemish areas is recent entrepreneurship, while Walloons have plenty of sources of "old money," often from mining businesses. This will influence the source of status in different parts of the country. In general, Belgians reward competence. This mentality is clearly evident to the visitor. Roads and buildings are sturdy and appear to be fit to stand a thousand years of wear. Food and drink are expertly prepared, second to none in the world. Social interaction is informal, particularly in Flemish areas, but even the Walloons have a less formal approach than the French.

An important aspect of the individual's outlook for both the Walloons and the Flemish is their negative image in France and the Netherlands. The Walloons are seen as slower and more mediocre (traits the French loathe and enjoy making fun of). The Flemish are seen as more rural and inward-looking than the worldly Dutch. This may be one clue to why the Belgians are so quick to embrace their new European identity. Their exposure to each other and other European countries, their affinity for compromise, and their remarkable language abilities make them perfectly suited to adopt this new European persona.

Belgium: Communication Style
As in all of Europe, and most of the world for that matter, it is a good idea to use formal address. There is a slight complication when we are dealing with Belgium, however. Calling a Walloon "Mr." or "Mrs." or a Flemish person "Monsieur" or "Madame" is just not a good idea. You should use English address for the Flemish and French for the Walloons. Having language options as part of the customer's ACD choices takes care of that dilemma.

Like the Dutch, the Belgians are averse to rank. That means anything that smacks of somehow trying to make yourself, your company, or country look better than your Belgian counterpart is not a good idea. Otherwise, Belgians are tolerant, flexible, and easy to deal with.

Denmark

Denmark is a relatively small country of about 5.5 million people located just north of Germany. Danish is a Germanic language, meaning it is related to German, English, and Swedish. Looking at a map, Denmark is made up of a series of islands and peninsulas. The Danish Vikings raided and traded all over Europe. Today, Denmark's economy is a mixture of agriculture, food processing, and a variety of other industries. The Danish landscape is relatively flat with rolling hills of meticulously maintained farmland. Denmark is firmly engaged in the economic and political unification of Europe, lacking any of the hesitation of its Scandinavian neighbors to the north.

Denmark is highly developed from every perspective, including telephone and computer infrastructure. Danes are also very educated and have a generally advanced ability to speak English, even when compared to their European neighbors. This fact has not gone unnoticed by several large companies such as SAP and Dell, who have located call centers in the Copenhagen area as part of a regional European strategy. Denmark also has labor laws that would generally be viewed by American companies as easier to deal with than those in, let's say, the Netherlands or Sweden. For example, Danish workers are allowed to work longer hours than their counterparts in Sweden.

Denmark: Cultural Analysis

Danes appear to be laid back, like the British. Their humor is also understated and sometimes sarcastic like British humor. The Danes value social equality, political democracy, and general modesty like their Scandinavian neighbors to the north. In business affairs they are thorough like their German neighbors to the south (though more lighthearted in their approach). In general, they are more passionate about life than their northern neighbors, whom they see as stiff.

Social welfare, equal rights, and quality of life are major themes in Danish social structure. While Danes value achievement in business, academia, and the arts, such success should not be flaunted (much like the Dutch). Whereas the Danes are careful not to project an image of superiority (one is put right back in his place, much like in the Netherlands), they actually have a tremendous confidence in their own abilities. This confidence goes beyond individual intellect to include their overall values of welfare and jovial way of life.

Denmark: Communication Style

The Danes have a very calm and humorous manner. Underneath, they are still related to their Scandinavian neighbors, so there is a streak of gloom in the Danes as well. For the Danes, this gloom has a different tone to it than Swedish or even Slavic melancholy. It is more of a practical realism. In other words, Danes do not romanticize the gloom.

As their neighbors to the south, Danes can care about detail, and like the Dutch they are no pushovers. You can't pull the rug over their eyes.

They are excellent negotiators, applying a combination of charm and sub-stance to strike a deal. You may drop formalities if you wish. Small talk and joking is appreciated.

France

France is an economic powerhouse of about sixty million people. It is a leader in agriculture, particularly, but also in various kinds of manufactur-ing and engineering, including telephony. When it comes to customer ser-vice, the French like to speak French. Perhaps, then, it should not come as a surprise then that the French call center industry is highly developed. An Ernst & Young study found that in the year 2000, there were 2,900 call cen-ters in France with more than ten employees. Interestingly, these were evenly distributed geographically across France.

The same survey revealed that 48 of those 2,900 call centers were bilin-gual. Make of that what you will, but my analysis is that French call centers are for French speakers in France. Nearly all of the 48 bilingual call cen-ters were in the Paris region. I speculate that they have some English capa-bility for foreigners in Paris and maybe some Arabic language options for that relatively large immigrant population. What is more, the call center industry in France is predicted to grow as companies are abandoning centralized and regionalized approaches in favor of outsourcing to local vendors.

Although I did not create a separate chapter in this book about French language global call center strategies, it should be said that there are 60 mil-lion French speakers in France, an additional 6.6 million in Canada, 4 mil-lion in Belgium, several million in Switzerland, and an additional 100,000 in Luxembourg. When we add Algeria, Morocco, Tunisia, several sub-Saharan countries such as Cote d'Ivoire and some tropical islands, we get between 77 million and 128 million French speakers, depending on how you count dialects and whether French is the first or the second language (http://www.fact-index.com/f/fr/french_language.html). The truth is that in dealing with French-language customer service, most of the activity will be in France. And, from my experience, if you want to do business in France, do it with French partners in France. If you want to consider outsourcing French customer service to Tunisia or Morocco, which does happen, I suggest you do it with French partners. The same goes for Canadians taking French calls—work with French partners to ensure that goes well. Another option is to consider Senegal as part of your French language options. The International Telecommunications Union has ranked Senegal as the top sub-Saharan country for quality of communications services. There are also incentives provided by regional development organizations there. Dakar is the capital and Senegal fortunately enjoys political stability.

I do not want to appear disrespectful when dealing French-language customer service. The fact is that we all want to speak our native tongue when getting customer support. So do the French, but perhaps even more so than other people. While it is not a stretch to ask a Dutch, German, Swedish, Czech, or Polish person to get customer service in English, at least just some of the time, could we do the same with the French? Sure, it is worth trying it. The problem is that you are going to offend them on some level. If you are willing to take that risk, route all those French callers to Manila and watch the abandon rate climb.

France: Cultural Analysis

It is important to understand that France is much higher on Hall's context scale than the United States and northern Europe (Hall 1990). This goes a long way in explaining the many misunderstandings between France and the rest of Europe and the world. Immersed in reminders of their rich and glorious history, the French relate contemporary issues to their historical origins. They make no secret of their belief that all things French are superior.

To this day, France is mired in a class structure in which social status is ascribed by socioeconomic family lineage—a hidden hierarchy with considerable hostility between groups. The French value intellectual precision and personal style. They loathe mediocrity. While outwardly they embrace diversity, the French have a certain level of fear regarding things foreign and different. They would never admit this, of course, but just dismiss those foreign things and lump them in with things mediocre to be made fun of. The French perception of time is anxious and urgent. They may seem rushed and fidgety at times.

A French schoolteacher was quoted as saying that the operating principle of French education is negative reinforcement (Hall 1990). French education emphasizes rhetoric and deductive reasoning. Academic standards are high. Discipline is strict. Emphasis is placed on eloquence of expression. Having produced some of the most significant philosophers in history, the French strive for truth and reason. However, the school system is inflexible and, some critics argue, does not prepare students for the complexities of modern life in France. Compared to other industrialized countries, very few—nearly all from the social elite—go to the best universities. Still, education is the gateway to a good job in the French economy, perpetuating status quo in the social structure.

The French management style is autocratic. Employees feel passionately about their directors. They love them or hate them, but they depend on them for direction. Rules and procedures are frequently disregarded in favor of more creative approaches or doing whatever works. French bureaucracies are notorious for their slowness and inefficiency.

France: Communication Style

While polite and formal, interaction among the French is more intense, emotional, and intimate that in most of the rest of Europe. They are more animated—they gesture with their bodies and offer facial expressions as they speak. The French are opinionated and don't always make good listeners, particularly when dealing with foreigners. You are encouraged to make your point quickly and logically (and don't forget to do it with wit and style)—and in French, of course.

A formula for success is to somehow demonstrate an appreciation for things French and to show a human side in terms of compassion, involvement, style, and intellect. This is a fine art that can quickly be misinterpreted as stereotypical, loud, and backslapping, especially coming from Americans. In some ways you are damned if you try and damned if you don't try. If you attempt a more reserved approach, you will likely be dismissed as stiff, boring, dull, and dim-witted. Maintain formality at all cost. Do not be the first to break the formality in your relationship.

Germany

Looking at a map, Germany occupies a large chunk of north-central Europe. Split in half after World War II, East and West Germany were reunified in 1990. Since then, Germany has carried a dual responsibility of rehabilitating the eastern portion Germany as well as helping to strengthen the economic development of all of Europe. The unified Germany is the world's third largest economy, with well over 80 million people. It excels in engineering and manufacturing, and it has one of the world's more technologically advanced telecommunications infrastructures and telecommunications industry as well.

The Saarland region in the southwest corner of Germany is a popular destination for call centers. It has a comparatively low cost of doing business and plenty of available labor. This has attracted companies such as America Online and Land's End.

Germany: Cultural Analysis

Time stands out when attempting to define German national character. Visitors are struck by the punctuality and general orderliness of German life. Germans see themselves as the most efficient and reliable people in the world. In fact, they feel a strong sense of responsibility toward both family and society at large.

Germany has undergone a transition from status being ascribed through family ties toward achieved status. Intellectual achievement earns the highest status. Status is expressed in outward appearances. For example, a strong emphasis is placed on titles. As in America, it is also acceptable to express success in the form of fancy cars and nice houses.

While Germans do take their work very seriously and may even appear gloomy at times, there is another side to the Germans. They take great care to create an atmosphere of *Gemütlichkeit*. While the direct translation of this word would be something like *cozy*, the word really implies a much richer combination of genuine hospitality and the deliberate creation of a safe, enjoyable space.

Germany is a very achievement-oriented country. Children are pushed hard to excel academically. Failing is a disaster. The ultimate goal is to pass the *Abitur*, a series of tests that determines a student's entry into the next level of schooling, the *Gymnasium*.

Germans value quality in everything. The focus is on procedures. They think in the longterm and have a problem with American monthly reports. Power is the name of the game in German business. You have to know where power is and how it is used. They play hardball, so if you don't, they will run right over you.

Germany: Communication Style

While Germans may appear businesslike in their interactions, this should not be interpreted as unfriendliness. Germans smile to show sincere affection, and since they don't mix their personal and business lives as much as Americans do, for example, smiles may seem rare in the work setting. They also do not appreciate exaggerations and hype.

Germans are quick to switch to English if needed. Their English is usually impeccable. For some reason, when Germans speak English on the telephone, it is very easy to understand. Germans tend to articulate and annunciate quite well even when they speak English. It also seems that they speak slightly more slowly and more deliberately.

By all means, maintain formal address. You should probably continue to use it even after they begin to call you by your first name, especially if they are older or carry big titles. If someone has a fancy degree, you must include the degree and the title in the address. For example, let's say I had a PhD in psychology and I worked as the human resources director at a company. You would address me as Herr Professor Direktor Granered. That is a mouthful, but that is how it works.

Privacy is important for Germans, so it is not a good idea to probe regarding personal matters. Germans form friendships based on common outlook and philosophy, so the personal details come much later in your interactions. By the way, friendships run very deep and last for a lifetime (very different from the American friendships). Be as honest as possible—Germans respect directness and truth. This can come in handy even in the call center. If you are empowered to do so, give an honest recommendation based on industry reports. Germans will value your input.

Written customer support and correspondence works wonderfully with Germans. Germans write well and enjoy keeping in touch. Never use Americanisms such as "the whole enchilada." This is true for any culture, but particularly with the Germans and French. From their perspective, it is informal, imprecise, and downright sloppy.

Italy

With Italy's roots in the Roman Empire, it may come as a surprise to some that the country of Italy was not formally created until 1861 (*World Fact Book* 2002). Located in southern Europe with Germany to the north and the Mediterranean Sea surrounding the boot-shaped southern portion, Italy is an economic powerhouse. Its economy is diverse, with industry gravitating to the north and agriculture to the south. Few people think of Italy as being in the same economic category as France and the United Kingdom, but it is. Serving Italian customers would best be done in Italy. Where to locate your call center will depend on your needs. There is a tremendous variation in skills and abilities between university graduates in Milan and workers in rural towns in the south of Italy, where unemployment can be as high as 20 percent. One skill they will all have is speaking Italian. From what I have heard, Italian is one of the easiest languages in the world to learn. First, we all can recognize so many of the words, no matter what our native tongues are. Second, the rules are clear and comparatively consistent. Last, the passion implicit in the language is contagious so that serves as a motivator. The bottom line is that there are no major Italian-speaking population centers outside Italy, and the penetration of English is not broad enough for you to assume that your customers will speak it.

Most call centers in Italy are located in the northern part of the country. Cities such as Turin and Piedmont have a rich industrial history and are thriving in everything from high technology to manufacturing. Labor costs will not be as reasonable as in other parts of the country, however.

Italy: Cultural Analysis

The Italians are optimists. They are flexible in their approach yet rigid in their beliefs. They are practical and at the cutting edge of modernity (look at their cars, telecommunications, fashion, and design) yet traditional, even parochial. While these traits seem like contradictions, they are not. Their national character is one that combines a secure identity with a confident purpose of direction. It is reflected in their art, not abstract contradictions that leave the observer wondering what the artist really meant but brilliantly clear expressions that capture the essence of an emotion, whether triumph or tragedy. That said, there are several subcultures in Italy that differ markedly from each other—from the German-speaking north to the island of Sicily.

As with other Latin cultures (and the Irish), fate is ultimately in the hands of God. The influence of the Catholic church is strong, mixed with a healthy dose of superstition. They see their connection with the past very clearly, meaning they are keenly aware of Italy's contributions to Western civilization. In dealing with them, you should know the size and importance of the Italian economy as it relates to rest of Europe. Their economy is larger than Great Britain's, so they are not a marginal player in any way. Italians, neither arrogant nor evangelical about their culture, do not have a complex.

Italy: Communication Style

Interaction deserves special attention when we look at Italian culture. Intimate, lively conversation is very important to Italians. The conversations may go on and on and take many turns along the way. Italians probably like talking even more than they like listening. They listen intently, but not 100 percent of the time, because they are very eager to make their next point. To do so, they have to think, and listening and thinking at the same time can be problematic. They have good manners, so they will usually not interrupt, but don't be offended if they do.

Face takes on a slightly different meaning in Italy than in Latin America and Asia. Italians are not overly sensitive or thin-skinned. You are allowed say what is on your mind, and there is no need to constantly praise them (give face). However, you have to be mindful of the relationships between the individual and the groups to which he or she belongs relating to both work and family. Those ties are strong, and what you say and do should not reflect badly on the extended group.

Italians are direct in their approach. They often do not understand the British style-coded speech of saying one thing and meaning another, sarcasm, and understatement for effect. As with other Latin cultures, your delivery, your appearance, and your wit all add up to a whole package—you. The Italian is watching "the whole deal." At that moment, nothing is more important than talking to you, including conversations on the phone. The importance of relationships over tasks certainly applies here.

Netherlands

The Kingdom of the Netherlands is a relatively small country in northwestern Europe with borders to Germany and Belgium to the east and south, and the North Sea to the west. Historically, the Netherlands was an important seafaring and trading power. It also was a colonial power, particularly in Indonesia, and an important early settlement community in North America. To this day, the Netherlands is outward-looking in its politics, particularly as it relates to Europe. It is a prosperous and open country. A little- known fact is that the Dutch rank third worldwide in value of agricultural exports, behind the United States and France. The Dutch are simply amazing in their ability to gain command of foreign languages, with 70 percent of the population speaking at least one foreign language (*World Fact Book* 2002). This has made the Netherlands a natural location for call centers intended to serve multiple European locations. I have heard stories of call centers using the thrills of Amsterdam as bait to attract youths with languages and technical skills from different locations in Europe. Whether there is any truth to this, I do not know. The thrills of Amsterdam aside, European labor laws allow a company to recruit workers from one country to another.

Netherlands: Cultural Analysis

The Dutch character is filled with paradoxes. Having a puritan heritage, they are perhaps the most permissive people in the world when it comes to topics such as drugs use and prostitution. Individualistic and achievement-oriented, they have a strong preference for moderation. They despise excess and those who flaunt it, while taking great pride in their national wealth and achievements as a country. While they hold humility and moderation as national virtues, they lament their small-country status.

As a low-context culture, status is achieved through hard work. As a feminine culture, there is emphasis on equality, which is reflected in their progressive social policies. Because the Dutch are individualistic and have a small power-distance, Americans, in particular, assume that the Dutch are just like them. There is one huge difference between Americans and the Dutch, however. Feminine values such as moderation, humility, and consensus are strong aspects of the Dutch outlook.

Dutch children are not pushed to achieve at an early age. Instead they are raised to be caring and accepting. The educational style is open-ended, meaning there is not always a right or a wrong answer to every question. The Dutch value hard work. At work, communication flows freely and decisions are reached through consensus. Buy-in from lower ranks is often obtained before making decisions.

Netherlands: Communication Style

When conversing in person, Dutch body language is reserved. Conversational style on the phone is also more concerned with the substance of what is being said than the experience of the conversation. That does not mean the interaction is unfriendly. It is efficient. The Dutch focus on the issue at hand and generally separate the issue from emotional attachment. That means making one's point in terms of fact rather than heated appeal will work much better.

Historically worldly and well-traveled traders, the Dutch are far from gullible. A colleague of mine once said about the Dutch that they have "very sensitive bullshit radar." That about sums it up. There is little room for nonsense, but in order to make that observation useful for you I have to define nonsense. *Nonsense* is excess, waste, bragging, flamboyance, anything over the top, pushiness, aggressiveness, salesmanship, one-sidedness, and insincerity. Stay away from those qualities, keep it real, keep it light, keep on task, and dealing with the Dutch is a true delight.

Sweden

A military power during the seventeenth century, Sweden has not participated in any war in almost two centuries. Sweden did not join the European Union until 1995 and decided to decline the euro in a national referendum in 1999. Sweden's long-successful economic formula of capitalism interlaced with substantial welfare elements has recently been undermined by high unemployment, rising maintenance costs, and a declining position in world markets. The country has a modern infrastructure that includes excellent internal and external communications and a skilled labor force.

This combination has not gone unnoticed by call center site selection experts. Sweden makes a very good location for serving the Scandinavian and Baltic region. There are also pools of highly trainable, English-speaking people in rural towns in Sweden, and community leaders and decision makers alike would be eager to talk to you about locating your call center in their community. Companies such as Hewlett-Packard, Sykes, SITEL, and DHL have set up shop in Sweden. Labor laws can be cumbersome, but Sweden might be worth a look.

Sweden: Cultural Analysis

Swedes enjoy two very different images around the world. One is the tall, soft-mannered, generally competent person who builds Volvos and Saabs for the world to enjoy. The other is a smug, annoying know-it-all who does not have the first clue about the reality of the world around him. Emotionally restrained and geographically remote, Swedes are perhaps not as worldly as most of their European neighbors. However, there are many qualities to like about the Swedes—a nurturing and peaceful outlook, a deep love of nature, and a nose for quality that goes well beyond engineering to include quality of life and quality of aesthetic and functional design.

As the most feminine country on Hofstede's dimensions, Sweden has a very progressive social system (Hofstede 1997). Every life is equally important. There is no deviation from this rule, and you would never convince a Swede otherwise. Achievement is important, but it happens on many levels. It is important not to overdo anything. *Lagom* is the rule—just right, not too much, and not too little. Once you have that big job with the big salary, you gladly give well over half of it in taxes, allowing the welder next door to also drive a Volvo and have a summer-house by a lake in the country just like you. The Social Democratic Party, which pioneered these social policies throughout the 1950s and 1960s, has enjoyed about half of the popular vote to this day.

Every culture sees itself as the norm and has limited insight as to how others see them. Swedes, however, have a particularly hard time stepping outside themselves to take a look. One reason for this may be that they are so very, very concerned with how other Swedes see them. This lack of an accurate self-image limits their ability to allow for cultural differences when dealing with diverse groups. There is a feeling here that the Swedish way of reason and compromise should always prevail.

Swedish children probably have more rights than adults in most other countries. It has happened on more than one occasion that a child who feels mistreated by a parent calls the police, and the police conduct a thorough investigation. Any physical or emotional abuse to a child is illegal, and children are informed of their rights through the school system. In addition, they enjoy one of the most developed day care and school systems in the world. Taking care of children is a serious matter—one of the highest priorities in Swedish society. Nothing is too good for Swedish children.

Swedes make decision by consensus. In addition, they avoid confrontation at any cost. This means that "getting to yes" can be a long, drawn out process. If you try to push them, they will abruptly adjourn the meeting and consult with one another about how to proceed, slowing down the process even further. One should also remember how difficult it is for a Swedish manager to push through results. It is very difficult for them to fire employees, and if they reward someone with a raise, most of it is taken out of the paycheck in the form of taxes. This leaves the Swedish manager without the benefits of the proverbial carrot and stick, having instead to rely on job knowledge and interpersonal rapport. Swedes are concerned with quality and on-time delivery more than profit.

Sweden: Communication Style

Swedes may appear emotionally reserved and even cold. Don't let this deter you. They have been likened to ketchup bottles—you have to shake them a few times before the ketchup comes out. Once it does, you will probably find a warm person who cares deeply about the world around him. Swedes are fairly informal with introductions. However, they stick to a respectful protocol in the course of a conversation. In person, this means you should stand up straight, maintain eye contact, listen actively, and speak clearly and intelligently (particularly in the workplace). If you take the same approach on the telephone, it will work wonders. It is almost a jumpy style that constantly affirms that you have heard and that you are listening.

Despite being firmly classified as low-context, Swedes do not like to be rushed or be put on the receiving end of any kind of pushy behavior. Time is important, but issues related to time must be handled politely. Should the conversation stall, don't worry or artificially push to the next topic. Swedes are a bit reflective like the Germans, and it does not bother them at all to ponder things for a moment.

If there is any decision making involved, remember that the Swede exists in a democratic and collaborative environment. He may need to deliberate with his colleagues before getting back to you.

11

Asian Cultures and Customer Service Options

This chapter focuses on call center options for servicing your customers in Asia. When we discussed India earlier, it was from the perspective of servicing English-speakers around the world. Of course, there are customers inside India and all over Asia. One way for Westerners to understand how to service customers in several Asian countries is to look at our approach to France. Just as you will be most successful providing customer service in France using French partners, the same is true for Korea and Japan. Both those countries have populations that are homogenous, and there are no other language options other than their native tongue. But don't make the Western mistake of thinking all Asian countries are the same. For contrast you need look no further than China. Chinese is spoken in China, Taiwan, Singapore, and in many sizable expatriate communities around the world. Therefore, your servicing options for Chinese customers are much broader.

Another variable here is the scale of the operation that you need. Let's say you are entering the Vietnamese market through a local distributor. You could probably serve your initial customers through an expatriate workforce from many cities in Asia and elsewhere. This may not work for Korea, as Korea's middle class is larger than Vietnam's. Economic growth in Korea also means that Koreans have not left their country in great numbers in recent history, so the first generation diaspora, which is what you are going to want for customer service, has a smaller footprint.

I admit that the discussion of Asian call center needs is not covered here with the same depth as Europe and North America. That certainly does not indicate a lack of appreciation for the current and future call center needs in China, India, Korea, Vietnam, Malaysia, Indonesia, and elsewhere in Asiaas economies grow and a middle class emerges rapidly. I think that models for serving Asian customers are emerging rapidly. While CRM enables call centers to add context to interactions anywhere, I think that this capability is particularly important when dealing with Asian cultures. The ability to provide context through past interaction, accent, consumer preference, and relationships can be very powerful in building relationships in these cultures. Learn from this chapter, but understand that this is a moving target, so if you want to be informed, you must constantly seek new and unique approaches.

China

A large and populous country like China is diverse in areas such as language, climate terrain, economic activity, and economic development. Most call center activity, whether taking inbound calls, outbound sales, or serving Chinese customers, will be in newly developed urban centers, such as Beijing, Shanghai, Guangdong, and Hong Kong.

An important fact to keep in mind when viewing the Chinese and how they see the world is to recognize that their civilization was well ahead of the rest of the world for centuries in premodern times. This is true in areas such as science, agriculture, art, and communication. In modern times, China has suffered famines, military defeat, foreign occupation, and brutal communist dictatorship.

More recent history is characterized by a pragmatic focus on economic development. As China continues to modernize and as its consumer market grows, the demand for telephone customer service for Chinese consumers will undoubtedly increase. China certainly does not come to mind when we list current call center powerhouses, however. Many companies have been able to serve Chinese speakers from places such as Singapore or Sidney, where it has been easier for Western consumer companies to operate.

There are many societal and cultural issues that influence the call center environment in China. Telephone infrastructure build-out is spotty and complicated by bureaucracy, affecting both your ability to reach customers and your call center location selection. The number of qualified agents available for hire to handle technical PC support, for example, is nowhere near what you would find in India or Malaysia. Even if you can overcome that issue, English language skills are not going to be at all what they are in India, meaning China is not really a good option for taking inbound English language calls.

The main reason for locating a call center here would be to support Chinese customers. And this is becoming increasingly important as the Chinese middle class grows and demands the same services Westerners expect in our daily lives. It is a good idea to establish relationships with a local partner to help you navigate the Chinese bureaucracy and to ensure that you are providing support in all the various Chinese dialects.

China: Cultural Analysis

Though suppressed during the Chinese Cultural Revolution in the 1960 and 1970s, the teachings of Confucius were officially reintroduced to Chinese society in the 1980s. Confucius was a scholar and a statesman from about 500 BC, who developed a series of principles for how people should get along with one another. They include themes like modesty, tolerance, patience, gratitude, and generosity. This philosophy of living has a pervasive influence on Chinese culture. In essence, these teachings seek *virtue* through acts. This markedly differs from the Western religious ideal of *truth*. In Chinese culture (and many other East Asian cultures that have been influenced by Chinese culture), there is no concept of absolute truth. Instead, things exist in relation to one another. Tangible and conceptual things are not separate either. If we think of Chinese medicine, in which mind and body affect each other, and events and conditions have physical manifestations. Extend this outlook to every aspect of life, and you may have a glimpse into how a Chinese person thinks.

The Chinese view their country, the Middle Kingdom, as the center of the universe. As the oldest civilization in the world, they believe they are far more evolved in every way than any foreigner. Understanding this is essential in understanding the Chinese, because it colors the way they look at you. This connection to China's long past also relates to their long-term orientation. Patience is important. Relationships take precedence over any short-term gain, and relationships take time to build.

It follows that the Chinese are very much group oriented, and saving face for all participants plays an important role in the social structure. Age plays an important role in Chinese society. Elders are shown respect and older people in business settings have more rank than younger colleagues. Decades of communist rule have led to communist party rank being important as well. With economic liberalization, achieved status is also emerging as a social force.

In addition to the teachings of Confucius, the teachings of Buddhism, and Taoism are also influential in Chinese life. While perhaps not practiced officially or openly, Buddhism certainly influences how the Chinese view spiritual matters. The goal in Buddhism is a state of liberty and ease that is achieved through detachment from the forces of fear and desire. The central theme of Taoism is the harmony of nature and mankind's role in that harmony.

Why have I introduced such heavy concepts in a book about call centers? Because I believe we Westerners do not have a fleeting chance of understanding eastern cultures without taking a close look at these themes. How can you begin to understand a person's beliefs and outlook if you are not willing to study the forces on which those beliefs are based? You can try, but your understanding will be superficial. Even a slight appreciation of these things will be helpful in agent–customer interaction in the call center.

China: Communication Style

The Chinese are more explicit and less introverted than the Japanese. Yet, there is still an element of implying the true meaning rather than stating it outright. Saving and giving face is also nearly as important in China as in Japan. Chinese people listen well and strive to accommodate you. The Chinese are reliable, and you can trust their decisions once they are reached. Their word is their bond. Chinese is more than just a language. It is a connection to their past. One will never be able to truly interact successfully with a Chinese-speaking person without full command of their language. From that perspective, it helps to realize what your status as a foreigner is and how age establishes a status relationship between you and the other person.

Japan

Japan is a hypermodern country with a keen sense of past. Since Japan's defeat in World War II, a combination of factors has led to the creation of the second largest economy in the world. These include: a constructive relationship with the United States, a strong focus on economic development from both government and industry, and a unique ability to combine Western methods and technologies with a traditional Japanese approach. The Japanese are as educated and trained in English language and Western culture as any group of people anywhere. Still, they want to receive call center support and services in their own language. Also, despite the fact that they have English skills, the cost of doing business in Japan does not make it a good site to provide offshore services to English-speaking customers. There is a small Korean minority, but beyond that the expatriate community is comparatively small. It is often recommended that customer support centers in Japan be split between at least two sites because of the risk of earthquakes. Also, because of the size and importance of the Japanese market, I recommend leaving little to chance. Identify good local partners who can help you get things done right. Since it is so expensive to do business in the major city centers in Japan, there are opportunities to be creative about where to locate the call center. Again, only a local partner would be able to navigate the nuances of the benefits of individual sites.

Japan: Cultural Analysis

While Japan is a very high-context culture, it has aspects that contradict high-context generalizations (much like the Dutch do as a low-context culture), making it difficult to analyze them with any precision. On the one hand, they are group oriented. On the other hand, they place strong emphasis on individual achievement. One has to always ask which one of these two strong motivators are prevalent at the moment—the ambitious, individualistic career person or the conformist who goes out of his way to save face for himself and his group.

It is hard to overstate the importance of face in Japanese life. It helps to think of face, or honor, as money. It can be saved. It can build up. Having it allows you to do things, meaning it grows like a good investment. Japanese are brought up to depend on groups, starting with family, school, and then company. Status in Japan is derived from two sources. One, it is ascribed through family. Two, it is achieved through hard work. As a whole, the Japanese are in-group oriented, meaning they make a sharp distinction between Japanese and foreigners, *gaijin*.

The Japanese see themselves as very honest. They keep their word and live up to their commitments. Losing face causes shame. Shame is a powerful force in the life of a Japanese individual. There is also conflict between the drive for individual achievement (and the fragmented life that results in modern society) and their tendency toward more holistic group orientation.

Japanese youths are pushed toward academic achievement at an early age. Failure causes shame for the family. In addition, school is a place where students learn to conform, to be Japanese. Schoolyard bullying is a very real problem in Japan, where children who are different are shunned and beaten severely, sometimes to their death. Despite open debate, it has been difficult for Japanese society to resolve this problem.

The Japanese work hard and log many hours. Japanese companies are managed hierarchically. Bosses serve as benevolent dictators with harmony as a goal. Though communication mostly takes place between equals, decisions are made with input from all levels of the organization. The pattern for this communication is complex and beyond the scope of this book. Status in a company depends on many things beyond individual achievement including age, education, and family.

Japan: Communication Style
The Japanese communication style is very indirect. They imply, leaving the listener to interpret. Their language is succinct and ambiguous. They stay

at a distance, more than arm's length, and keep nonverbal animation to a minimum. They are listening to more than your words.

If you are taking calls from Japanese customers in English, understand that face is everything to the Japanese. That means all the rules regarding the hidden no's all apply. If you have a scheduled conference call, or other appointment, call on time. The Japanese are time conscious. That does not mean, however, that the Japanese are pushy and results oriented. They allow events to flow. If there is no final decision or resolution, it does not mean the end of the world is near. Beyond those hints, you probably have to be Japanese to understand the nuances of nonverbal cues. Synch with them the best that you can. Allow them to take the lead. Try not to feel uncomfortable during silent pauses, and take a gentle approach in general.

Singapore

Singapore is an island tucked between Malaysia and Indonesia. It was a British colony until 1963, when it joined Malaysia only to become independent two years later (*World Fact Book* 2002). Trade and entrepreneurship are the cornerstones of Singapore's flourishing economy. It is politically stable and free of corruption. Singapore exports a variety of products and services. It is particularly suitable as a call center location for several reasons. First, it is stable and developed so it is generally easy to do business there. Second, it has an highly developed telephone infrastructure. Third, it has language facility in English and Chinese, primarily, but also in a wide variety of other languages from expatriate communities and their families. All these wonderful things come at a price, however. Singapore is not the least expensive place to locate your call center.

Singapore: Cultural Analysis

While Singapore is made up of four ethnic groups (plus businesspeople from every corner of the world), the population of this small island is predominantly of Chinese origin (75 percent plus). Both its position as a trading outpost and 120 years of British rule influence the national character. The people take a pragmatic approach and are generally outward looking in their view of the world. This is balanced with traditional Chinese Confucian values such as humility and reliability. English is the language of business in Singapore.

While family lineage is an important part of the identity of a person from Singapore, status is achieved through hard work, evidenced by monetary reward. Business associations are built on personal relationships based on trust.

The story of Singapore is the story of an economic miracle. Whereas the country is officially a parliamentary democracy, it has been ruled by the same party since its independence in 1965. Financial wealth and social order take precedence over social and political freedoms. This unspoken social contract colors the individual's outlook. Why debate political reform when there is no crime and ample economic opportunity?

Work and career are very important. To participate in the economic miracle is to be Singaporean. Making money is also important. Power distance is large, meaning accept authority and expect clear directions. As in other Chinese-influenced cultures, this large power distance is tempered with humble and consultative approaches to doing business.

Singapore: Communication Style

As if you needed more reasons to put Singapore on your short list of places to put your call center, Singaporeans make excellent listeners. They listen patiently, and if they disagree, they will let you know of their disagreement politely (allowing you to save face). To communicate effectively, the outsider should take a similar approach. Allow people to finish what they are saying, including a slight pause. This is polite. Validate what they are saying. Avoid saying "no." Rejecting their ideas is equivalent to rejecting who they are. You should explore more roundabout ways of arriving at a consensus. Smiles and uncomfortable laughs are ways to hide embarrassment.

This next idea may be common sense for most of us, but it may be particularly important to use good manners when dealing with customers from Singapore. You should never interrupt or finish people's sentences for them. This is pushy, and pushy is not good. Boasting and bragging are frowned upon as well. A glimpse into their perspective on manners is their law on chewing gum in public. Until recently, it was completely illegal.

Now, the law has been relaxed. It is just that those who want to indulge have to give their names and "produce identification" (whatever that is), and they can buy gum only at the pharmacy.

Balance soft manners with firm principles. They will respect you for both. Hesitation and uncertainty are traits of weakness, and if there is any negotiation involved in the situation, they might take advantage of you. A quick win is to compliment them on their economic achievements.

Conclusion

I want to conclude this book with a case study from a Peppers & Rogers white paper called "Customer Relationship Management in Asia: A Cross Cultural Case Study Based on Aetna Universal Insurance" (Berhad 2002). In short, Aetna purchased a Malaysian life insurance company named Universal Life in the early 1990s. Universal Life had thrived by motivating agents with high commissions, which attracted agents with wide networks of friends and family to leverage its contacts to sell insurance services. After the takeover, Universal Life underwent a series of rationalizations that included cuts in commissions, causing disruption to this personal network infrastructure. Agent attrition meant customers lost.

This blunder is not so surprising. Aetna is not the first corporation to lose business as a result of not having a full understanding of how business gets done in a foreign culture. What is surprising is the sophistication of Aetna's comeback strategy, which is a lesson in how to do it right. It integrates old and new, east and west, and offers hope to us all that a holistic and creative perspective is possible.

First, ING Aetna (Aetna was purchased by ING in 2001) launched a marketing campaign to reverse the perception that insurance companies are quick to take people's money and reluctant to give it back. Second, they offered office space to agents at the company. In other words, there was a physical connection between Aetna and the agent. Third, they implemented a CRM solution that took previously isolated customer data regarding life, property, casualty, and health insurance information, integrated it, and made it available to agents. Now ING Aetna agents could interact with customers from offices physically located in Aetna buildings with a full awareness of the customer's life situation and insurance needs. Loan application processes were overhauled with "customer outcomes first" in mind. That meant the first priority was *who* was applying for the loan and why—not abstract bureaucracy and paperwork. Personifying the experience and applying technology integration greatly reduced loan processing time. Last on the list of improvements was the call center. Whereas requests submitted through an agent had previously been subjected to delays, now they were processed with highest priority, leading to even greater customer satisfaction.

This is the kind of thinking that is going to work across many industries. It adapts Western technology to a local setting, creating a high-context experience for a high-context customer, while delivering service at a speed that was previously unthinkable. Like so many other companies, Aetna had to go through a painful learning curve before arriving at a true solution. You can shorten the learning curve and arrive at solutions that are better than anything you can imagine at this time. When we keep both customer and company outcomes in mind, when we listen, learn, plan, train, and execute with patience and awareness, anything is possible.

References

"100 Cool Call Center Things." 2000. *Call Center Magazine*, 5 October.

Allen, Mark. 2002. *The Corporate University Handbook: Designing, Managing, and Growing a Successful Program*. New York: Amacom.

Angrawal, Vivek. 2003. "Offshoring: Is It a Win-win Game?" *McKinsey Global Institute*, August.

Anton, Jon, et al. 2002. "Improving Call Center Performance Through Optimized Site Selection." Santa Maria, CA: Benchmarkportal, Inc.

Berhad, H. and Tim Tyler. 2002. "Customer Relationship Management in Asia: A Cross Cultural Case Study based on Aetna Universal Life Insurance." *Pepper & Rogers Group*, January.

Brislin, Richard W. 1981. *Cross-Cultural Encounters*. New York: Pergamon Press.

"Call Centers in EMEA to 2007." 2002. http://www.datamonitor.com. 2 October.

Cleveland, Brad and Julia Mayben. 2001. *Call Center Management on Fast Forward*. Annapolis, MD: Call Center Press.

"Computers: New Considerations." 2004. *Consumer Reports*. June.

Craig, Robert L. 1996. *The ASTD Training and Development Handbook: A Guide to Human Resource Development*. New York: McGraw Hill.

Crouch, Ned. 2004. *Mexicans and Americans: Cracking the Cultural Code*. Yarmouth, ME: Intercultural Press.

Cultureactive Country Reports. 2000. http://www.cultureactive.com.

Datamonitor. "Global Offshore Call Center Outsourcing: Who will be the next India?" 2003. *datamonitor.com*, 19 December.

Davies, Paul. 2004. *What's This India Business?* Yarmouth, ME: Intercultural Press.

Davis, Bob. "Finding Lessons of Outsourcing in 4 Historical Tales." *Wall Street Journal*, 29 March.

Dawson, Keith. 2001. *The Call Center Handbook*. Berkley, CA: CMP Books.

Drucker, Jesse. 2004. "Global Talk Gets Cheaper." *Wall Street Journal*. 11 March.

Durr, William. 2001. *Navigating the Customer Contact Center in the 21st Century*. Boston, MA: Advanstar Communications.

"Executive Planet Country Reports." 2002. http://www.executiveplanet.com.

"Global Offshore Call Center Outsourcing: Who will be the next India?" 2003. http://www.datamonitor.com . 19 December.

Field, Anne. 2004. "Corporate America's Learning Curve." *Fortune Magazine*. 3 June.

Fiorina, Carly. 2004. "Be Creative, Not Protectionist." *Wall Street Journal*, 13 February.

Fox, Nicols, 2004. "The Case Against Efficiency." *Washington Post.* 15 February.

Hall, Edward T. and Mildred Reed Hall. 1990. *Understanding Cultural Differences: Germans, French, and Americans.* Yarmouth, ME: Intercultural Press.

Edward T. Hall, 1958. *The Silent Language.* New York: Anchor Books.

———. 1977. *Beyond Culture.* New York: Anchor Books.

———. 1983. *The Dance of Life.* New York: Anchor Books.

———. 1990. *Hidden Differences: Doing Business With the Japanese.* New York: Anchor Books.

Hofstede. Geert. 1997. *Cultures and Organizations: Software of the mind.* New York: McGraw-Hill.

Kirkpatrick, Donald. L. 1998. *Evaluating Training Programs: The Four Levels.* San Fransisco, CA: Berrett-Koehler.

Lampton, Bill. 2003. "Paragon of Customer Service Excellence—The Ritz-Carlton Hotel." http://www.expertmagazine.com, 1 December.

Levin, Greg. 2002 "Indian Outsourcing Firms Set for Explosive Growth." *Call Center Management Review.* September.

Mathew, James and Arshdeep Sehgal. 2003. "Dell Setting Up Second Subsidiary in India." *The Economic Times Online,* 29 December.

McCarthy, John C. 2004. Near-Term Growth of Offshoring Accelerating: Resizing US Services Jobs Offshore, Executive Summary. Forrester Research. *http://www.forrester.com,* 4 May.

Meisler, Andy. 2004. "Think Globally, Act Rationally." *Workforce Management,* January.

Morrisson, Terri et al. 1995. *Kiss, Bow, or Shake Hands: How to Do Business in Sixty Countries.* Holbrook, MA: B Adams.

Morse, Dan. 2004. "Kentucky Answered the Call of the Future—But Got Bad News." *Wall Street Journal,* 9 March.

"Outsourcing 101." 2004. *Wall Street Journal Editorial,* 27 April.

Parks, Bob. "Where the Customer Service Rep. is King." *Business 2.0.* June.

Phillips, Michael M. 2004. "Outsourcing Fears Land in Congress's Lap." *Wall Street Journal,* 5 March.

Read, Brendan. 2002. "A Murky New Dawn for EMEA Call Centers." *Call Center Magazine.* 7 July.

———. 2002. "Riding the Outsourcing Wave." *Call Center Magazine.* 4 August.

———. 2002. "Slow but Steady Course for the Asia Pacific." *Call Center Magazine,* 4 November.

———. 2002. "The Ultimate Balancing Act." *Call Center Magazine.* 6 May.

Sento Corporation. 2003. "Case Study: Intuit." *ContactCenterworld.com,* 28 May.

Sugrue, Brenda. 2003. *State of the Industry Report 2003: ASTD's Annual Review of U.S. and International Trends in Workplace Learning and Performance*. Arlington, VA: American Society for Training and Development, 1 November.

"TCS Unaffected by Lehman's Cancellation of Wipro Deal." 2003. *India Times: The Economic Times Online*, 17 December.

"U.K. Firm to Shut Down India Call Centre, Transfer Jobs Back." 2004. *India Times: The Economic Times Online*, 26 January.

"Vertical Guide to Call Centers in EMEA." 2004. http://www.datamonitor.com. 21 April.

Weaver, Gary. 1987. "Contrast Cultures Continuum." *Readings in Cross-Cultural Communication*. Lexington, MA: Ginn Press.

——. 1988–1989. *Various lectures in cross-cultural communication*. Washington, D.C.: The American University School of International Service.

World Fact Book. 2002. The Central Intelligence Agency. Langley, VA.

Index